Guiding Your Teen

Essential Conversations That Matter Before High School

Janice A. Campbell

© Copyright 2024 - All rights reserved.

The content contained within this book may not be reproduced, duplicated or transmitted without direct written permission from the author or the publisher.

Under no circumstances will any blame or legal responsibility be held against the publisher, or author, for any damages, reparation, or monetary loss due to the information contained within this book, either directly or indirectly.

Legal Notice:

This book is copyright protected. It is only for personal use. You cannot amend, distribute, sell, use, quote or paraphrase any part, or the content within this book, without the consent of the author or publisher.

Disclaimer Notice:

Please note the information contained within this document is for educational and entertainment purposes only. All effort has been executed to present accurate, up to date, reliable, complete information. No warranties of any kind are declared or implied. Readers acknowledge that the author is not engaged in the rendering of legal, financial, medical or professional advice. The content within this book has been derived from various sources. Please consult a licensed professional before attempting any techniques outlined in this book.

By reading this document, the reader agrees that under no circumstances is the author responsible for any losses, direct or indirect, that are incurred as a result of the use of the information contained within this document, including, but not limited to, errors, omissions, or inaccuracies.

ISBN# 979-8302018908

Contact author: wealthhealthforever@hotmail.com

Table of Contents

Introduction

Chapter 1: Opening the Lines of Communication

  Choosing the Right Place, Time, and Situations for Conversation

    Choosing a Private Space

    Timing Matters

    One-on-One Conversations

  Communication Is Essential for Healthy Relationships

    Assuring Teens of Confidentiality

    Reflecting on the Past

    Emphasizing Your Intentions

    Showing Genuine Interest

    Building Confidence Through Dialogue

  Listening Without Judgment

    The Art of Active Listening

    Avoiding Interruptions

    Thanking Them for Their Honesty

    The Impact of Nonjudgmental Listening

    Building Trust Through Consistent Listening

    Acknowledging Their Feelings

  Bridging the Gap: Sharing Your Own Experiences

Assuring Them: "I've Been Where You Are"

Sharing Your Decisions as a Teen

Discussing Your Struggles and Successes

Reflecting on Regrets

Encouraging Open Dialogue

Chapter 2: Be Trustworthy

The Foundation of Trust: Truthfulness and Honesty

Inviting the Conversation: "Do You Trust Me?"

Apologizing When Trust Is Broken

The Promise of Honesty

The Impact of Trust on Communication

Building Trust Through Consistency

Leading by Example

Encouraging Honesty Through Acceptance and Support

Acceptance: The First Step to Honesty

Commending Honesty: A Positive Reinforcement

Managing Your Reactions: Staying Calm and Collected

Discussing Mistakes: Focus on Solutions, Not Punishment

Navigating Repentance: Acknowledging Feelings of Guilt

Collaborating on Solutions: Learning Together

- Establishing Ground Rules: A Framework for Honesty
- Creating a Culture of Openness
- Building Trustworthiness: Earning Respect Together
  - Addressing Past Honesty Issues: A Constructive Approach
  - Setting Goals for Improvement: Collaborating on Next Steps
  - Building Respect Through Consistency and Reliability
  - Encouraging Open Dialogue: The Importance of Mutual Respect
  - Building a Culture of Trust and Respect
- Trust and Freedom: Earning Privileges Together
  - Engaging Your Teen in the Conversation
  - Setting Clear Expectations and Next Steps
  - Providing Guidance and Support
  - Celebrating Progress and Building Trust
  - The Balance of Trust and Responsibility
- Keep Your Promises
- Start With a Clean Slate

Chapter 3: Be Reliable

- Teen's Expectations of Parents
  - What Are Parents Providing Reliably?
  - Where Can Parents Improve?

- What Are the Privacy Boundaries Teens Want Respected?
- Parent's Expectations of Teens
  - Teens Should Be Forthcoming About Where They Go and With Whom
  - Teens Are Expected to Be Home by Supper Time Each Day
  - Teens Are Expected to Keep Their Room Clean and Neat
  - Teens Are Expected to Complete Their Chores
  - Parents Should Discuss Any Other House Rules the Teen Is Expected to Abide By
- Know the Parents of Your Teen's Friends
  - Do You Share the Same Moral Standards?
  - Do They Instill Their Moral Standards in Their Teens?
  - Do They Have Meaningful Conversations With Their Teens?
  - Do They Allow Their Teen Privileges and Freedoms That You Do Not?
  - What Sort of Example Are They Setting for Their Teen?
- Chapter 4: Alcohol
  - Do You Drink to Excess or to the Point of Getting Drunk?
    - Do You Indulge in Alcohol Every Day?

Do You Always Serve Alcohol to Your Adult Guests?

Do You Need to Make Changes to Improve the Example You Are Setting?

Managing Alcohol in the Home: Setting Boundaries and Trusting Your Teen

Is Alcohol a Temptation for Your Teen?

Taking Precautions: Locking Alcohol Away or Removing It

Commending Responsible Behavior

Alcohol: Understanding the Risks and Talking With Your Teen

Explaining the Dangers of Alcohol to Your Teen

Discussing Alcohol Use Among Your Teen's Friends

Addressing Peer Pressure: How Did It Make You Feel?

Evaluating Friendships: Are They a Good Influence?

Preparing for Future Scenarios: What If It Happens Again?

Open Conversations About Alcohol Use

Commend Your Teen for Their Honesty

Addressing a Potential Alcohol Problem

Reassure Your Teen of Your Love and Support

Commending Self-Control

- Allowing Controlled Exposure to Alcohol at Home
  - Helping Teens Resist Peer Pressure
  - Setting Clear Boundaries
- Discussing Consequences for Unauthorized Alcohol Consumption

Chapter 5: Dating
- The Influence of Hormones
  - Offering Guidance and Support
  - Taking Dating Off the Table
- The Benefits of Group Activities Over One-on-One Dating
  - The Safety in Numbers
  - Setting Boundaries and Protecting Your Teen
  - Aiding Emotional Development
  - Long-Term Benefits
- Early Awareness and the Reality of Premarital Sex
  - Addressing the Temptations and Pressures
  - Real-Life Conversations With Your Teen
  - Guiding Toward Long-Term Perspective

Chapter 6: Drugs
- Understanding Local Drug Availability and Dangers
  - How to Get Information About Drugs in Your Area
  - Common Street Names and Symptoms of Drugs
  - Recognizing Symptoms of Drug Use

- Educating Teens on the Dangers of Experimenting With Drugs
  - Explaining the Immediate Risks
  - The Slippery Slope of Addiction
  - The Long-Term Health Consequences
  - Peer Pressure and Social Consequences
  - Encourage Open Communication and Support
- Helping Your Teen Break Free From Drug Addiction
  - Determining Your Teen's Willingness to Quit
  - Seeking Professional Help
- Assessing Your Teen's Efforts to Break Free From Drugs
  - Has Your Teen Tried to Quit?
  - Seeking Professional Help
  - If They Haven't Tried to Quit
  - Supporting Their Journey

Chapter 7: Choice of Friends

- Knowing Your Teen's Friends
  - Getting to Know Their Friends' Parents
  - Helping Your Teen Assess Friend Influences
  - Recognizing Positive and Negative Influences
  - Encouraging Healthy Friendships
- Encouraging Wholesome Friendships
  - Create a Welcoming Home Environment
  - Make Your Home a Safe Haven

    Be Hospitable and Prepared

    Organize Sleepovers and Slumber Parties

    Promote Positive Friendships

Chapter 8: Changes in Your Body

  Understanding Natural Changes

    Boys and Their Transformations

  Embracing Privacy: A Teen's Need for Space

    The Importance of Personal Space

    Establishing Trust Through Confidentiality

    Finding the Balance

  Facilitating Open Conversations: The Power of Shared Experience

    The Comfort of Same-Sex Discussions

    Sharing Your Own Experiences

    Normalizing the Experience

    Building a Supportive Atmosphere

  Shopping Together: A Bonding Experience

    Supporting Girls: A Visit to the Store

    Guiding Boys: The Essentials

    A Fashion Adjustment: Updating the Wardrobe

Chapter 9: Peer Pressure

  The Need to Be Accepted

  Navigating Peer Pressure: Questions for Reflection

    Reflecting on Influences

Honesty in Friendships

The Pressure to Deceive

Empowering Decision-Making

Helping Your Teen Navigate Peer Pressure

Anticipate the Problem

Think About the Pros and Cons

Decide What You Will Do

Act on Their Decision

Is Your Teen Dealing With Bullying?

Recognizing Signs of Distress

Starting the Conversation

Understanding the Nature of Bullying

Helping Your Teen Build Self-Esteem and Confidence

Acknowledging Resilience in the Face of Pressure

The Power of Affirmation

Chapter 10: Pornography

Dealing With the Complex World of Teen Curiosity

Don't Be Shocked—Curiosity Is Natural

The Reality Check: Pornography Isn't Harmless

Understanding the Consequences

The Emotional Toll

Building a Healthy Relationship With Intimacy

Encouraging Your Teen to Move Beyond Pornography

Understanding Their Willingness to Change
Reasons Behind Their Hesitation
The Conversation About Consequences
If They're Ready to Let Go
Digital Clean-Up: Taking Action Together
Installing Parental Filters: A Proactive Approach
Embracing Wholesome Activities With Your Teen
- Plan an Exciting Family Vacation
- Quality One-on-One Time
- Something Is Revitalizing
- Encouraging New Hobbies
- Creating a Balanced Lifestyle

Chapter 11: Setting Goals
Helping Your Teen Dream Big
Breaking Down Long-Term Goals
- Encourage Goal Setting
- Explore Academic Opportunities
- Develop Personal Traits
- Utilize Free Time Wisely

Breaking Away From Unwanted Habits
- Identify Personal Habits
- Tackle Procrastination
- Reliability in Responsibilities

Exploring New Hobbies

- Mastering Basic Life Skills
- Building Responsibility With Babysitting
- Managing Money Wisely
- The Benefits of a Part-Time Job

The Power of Time Management
- Creating a Summer Schedule
- Sticking to the Schedule

Chapter 12: Sex

Your Role in Sexual Education

Encouraging Chastity: A Path to Emotional and Physical Safety
- Emotional Scars and Broken Hearts
- The Reality of Unwanted Pregnancy
- The Health Risks: STIs and Lifelong Illnesses
- The Impact of Promiscuity and Reputation
- Building Self-Respect and Self-Esteem
- Open the Door for Discussion

Navigating the Pressure: Understanding Consent and Choice
- Recognizing Peer Pressure
- The Role of Friends
- Understanding the Implications of Birth Control
- Fostering Self-Respect and Self-Esteem

Chapter 13: Smoking

Acknowledge the Reality of Smoking

Review the Facts Together

The Impact on Relationships and Self-Image

Secondhand Smoke: Protecting the People Around Them

Talking About Vaping

Encourage Open Dialogue

Be a Support System

Leading by Example

Step 1: Determine If Your Teen Is Willing to Stop

Asking the Right Questions

Step 2: Determine If They Need Help

Step 3: Helping Them Quit on Their Own

Developing a Quit Plan

Step 4: Lead by Example

Step 5: Offer Your Unconditional Support

Encourage Your Teen to Stay Resolute in Their Decision Not to Smoke

Encourage Your Teen to Write Down Their Reasons for Not Smoking

Commend Your Teen for Being Honest and Seeking Your Support

Encourage Your Teen to Set a Quit Date

Help Your Teen Get Rid of All Cigarettes, Lighters, Matches, and Ashtrays

Remind Your Teen That Withdrawal Symptoms Are Temporary, but the Rewards Are Permanent

    Encourage Your Teen to Avoid Situations and People That Will Tempt Them to Smoke

    Celebrate Small Wins Along the Way

Chapter 14: Social Media

    Help Your Teens Appreciate the Risks Associated With Social Media

        Once Something Is Posted, It Can't Be Permanently Erased

        Private and Personal Information Is Out There for Anyone to Access

        Teach Your Teen About Digital Footprints

        Cyberbullying and Online Harassment Are Real Threats

        Social Media Can Impact Mental Health

        Encourage Positive Social Media Use

        Set Boundaries and Screen Time Limits

Is Your Teen Addicted to Social Media or the Internet?

    How Much Time Does Your Teen Spend on Their Devices?

    Does Your Teen Neglect Other Activities?

    Has Your Teen's School Performance Suffered Since Getting a Smartphone?

    Is Your Teen Texting During Meals or Interrupting Conversations?

    Are Teachers Noticing Social Media Use in Class?

- Helping Your Teen Find a Healthy Balance
  - Encourage Your Teen to Set Reasonable Limits
  - Recognize the Need for Connection
  - Discourage Gossip and Inappropriate Media Use
  - Is Media Use Impacting Their Schoolwork or Sleep?
  - Encourage Accountability: Keeping Track of Screen Time
  - Sticking to Media Time Limits
  - Helping Your Teen Create a Balanced Relationship With Media
- Chapter 15: Suicide
  - Is There an Apparent Reason for the Sadness or Depression?
    - Assure Your Teen You've Noticed a Change in Their Mood
    - The Problem Won't Go Away, But Talking About It Helps
    - Assure Your Teen That Their Privacy Will Be Respected
    - Remind Your Teen That Time Brings Change
    - Do Mental Health Problems Run in Our Family?
  - Consider Seeking Professional Help
    - Remind Your Teen: There Is No Shame in Seeking Medical Help
    - Understanding the Signs of Struggle

    Sharing Your Own Challenges
    Building a Support Network
    Creating a Safe Environment
    Encourage Journaling as an Outlet
    Draw Close to God in Prayer
    Encouraging Positive Activities
    Remind Them of Your Unconditional Support

Conclusion

References

Introduction

As a parent of a preteen or teen, you know that these years can be a challenging mix of excitement, confusion, and worry. Your child is on the brink of adolescence, a time filled with rapid changes and new experiences. You might find yourself asking, *How do I connect with my teen? How can I help them navigate peer pressure, set positive goals, and protect them from the dangers of drugs, alcohol, and other risky behaviors?*

You're not alone in feeling overwhelmed by these questions. Many parents grapple with how to create a safe space for open communication, especially regarding difficult topics. As a caring parent, you want to ensure your child feels supported, understood, and prepared to face the challenges ahead.

In *Guiding Your Teen: Essential Conversations that Matter Before High School*, we delve into these pressing questions, offering you practical guidance and thoughtful strategies for fostering meaningful conversations with your child. Here are just a few of the key questions we will explore together:

- **How do I open the lines of communication with my teen?** This foundational step is important for creating an environment where your child feels comfortable sharing their thoughts and feelings.

- **How can I help my teen combat negative peer pressure?** We'll discuss effective techniques to empower your teen to stand firm against the influences of their peers.

- **What conversations should I prioritize with my teen?** Understanding what matters most in your child's life can help you guide them effectively.

- **How do I protect my teen from sex, drugs, alcohol, smoking, pornography, and suicide?** We'll look at how to address these difficult topics head-on, equipping you to speak with confidence and compassion.

- **How do I encourage my teen to set reasonable, positive life goals?** Together, we'll explore ways to inspire your child to dream big while staying grounded in reality.

- **How do I prepare my teen for the changes in their body?** With so much happening physically and emotionally, it's important to navigate these changes thoughtfully.

We recommend starting with Chapters 1 through 3 in order, as they lay the groundwork for the following discussions. Each chapter builds upon the previous one, creating a solid foundation for open dialogue. The subsequent chapters can be explored in any order that feels most relevant to you and your teen's unique circumstances.

Parenting teens can feel daunting, especially when you consider the pressures and temptations surrounding them. You can experience frustration when your teen seems closed off or disinterested or fear when you think about the risks they face in today's world. This book recognizes those feelings and offers support, insights, and practical advice to help you navigate this challenging terrain.

By reading *Guiding Your Teen*, you will gain the tools you need to foster trust and connection with your child. You will learn how to engage in the vital conversations that can influence their decisions and help them thrive during these formative years. You will feel more empowered as a parent, ready to tackle tough topics and create an environment where your teen feels valued and understood.

You'll find that this book speaks directly to you because I understand your challenges.

By investing your time in this book, you are taking a proactive step towards nurturing a healthy, open relationship with your teen. You'll discover creating a space for meaningful conversations that matter before high school and beyond is possible.

So, let's embark on this journey together, empowering your teen to navigate adolescence with confidence, clarity, and resilience. This is the right book for you, and I'm honored to guide you through it.

Chapter 1: Opening the Lines of Communication

Nothing in life is more important than the ability to communicate effectively. -Gerald R. Ford

Imagine this: your teen comes home from school with earbuds in, scrolling through their phone with an expression that says, "Don't bother me." You want to talk about something important, but how do you break through that barrier? The reality is that opening the lines of communication with your teen can feel like navigating a minefield. However, creating a solid connection with your child is important, especially as they approach the challenging high school years.

Let's explore how you can create a comfortable environment that fosters open dialogue. First, it's integral to understand that communication isn't just about talking; it's about engaging in a way that your teen feels safe and respected. The foundation of meaningful conversations begins with the right choice of place, time, and situation.

Choosing the Right Place, Time, and Situations for Conversation

When it comes to talking with your teen, choosing the right setting can make all the difference. Start by asking your teen when and where they would like to talk. This simple question shows them that you value their preferences and are willing to meet them halfway. It could be a spot in the living room or even during a walk in the park. By giving them a say in the matter, you're already setting the stage for a more open and inviting conversation.

You can ask your daughter, "Hey, when would be a good time to chat? Would you prefer to talk over dinner or maybe during our weekend hike?" Such questions signal to her that you are approachable and that her input is valued.

Choosing a Private Space

Next, consider the physical space where the conversation will take place. Privacy is a must-have when discussing sensitive topics. Think about a car ride after school; it can be a perfect opportunity for a heart-to-heart. The relaxed atmosphere, combined with the shared experience of driving, can help your teen feel less pressured. They may open up more easily when you're side by side rather than facing each other directly.

Another good option is talking after supper in their room. Many teens feel more comfortable in their personal space, surrounded by their belongings, where they can express themselves freely. Creating that intimate setting can encourage your teen to share their thoughts without feeling exposed or judged.

Timing Matters

Timing is equally important when initiating conversations. You want to find moments when your teen is not distracted. For instance, if they're in the middle of their homework, they may not be receptive to a deep conversation about relationships or their future. Similarly, movie time with friends may not be the best moment to dive into heavy topics.

Instead, aim for times when you find your teen alone and in a good mood. A casual evening when they seem relaxed, maybe while grabbing a snack or after they've finished a video game session, can be ideal. Keep in mind that initial conversations should be brief and non-confrontational. You don't need to dive deep right away; sometimes, just touching on a topic can be enough to lay the groundwork for more extensive discussions later.

One-on-One Conversations

Additionally, a one-on-one conversation with the parent of the same sex can be a comforting starting point for many teens. For example, if you're a dad, sitting down with your son may feel less intimidating than talking to his mom. Each teen is different, and some may feel more comfortable discussing certain subjects with a parent of the same gender.

This isn't to say that a conversation with the opposite-sex parent is off-limits; rather, it's about recognizing what may feel easier for your teen. If your daughter has a question about relationships, she might feel more at ease speaking with you if you're her mom, or vice versa.

Stop here and think about your experiences. *When did you feel most at ease talking to your own parents? Was it a moment shared while cooking together, or perhaps while doing an activity you both enjoyed?* These relatable instances can resonate with your kids when they see you are trying to make an effort to connect.

Communication Is Essential for Healthy Relationships

Communication forms the backbone of healthy relationships, especially between you and your teens. As your child deals with the complex journey of adolescence, fostering an environment where they feel comfortable expressing themselves becomes critical. To build that kind of atmosphere, you must actively work to assure your teen that anything discussed will remain private. This assurance is key to establishing trust and openness.

Assuring Teens of Confidentiality

When your teen shares something personal—whether it's about a friendship issue or something they're struggling with at school—the last thing you want is for them to feel exposed. Begin by clearly communicating that your discussions will remain confidential. You can say, "I want you to know that whatever we talk about stays between us. You can trust me." This simple reassurance can create a safe space for your teen to open up, knowing that their thoughts and feelings are respected and protected.

Think about how often you might feel vulnerable when discussing personal matters. Now, imagine the relief your teen would feel knowing they can speak freely without fear of judgment or having their privacy violated. This trust can be a game-changer in encouraging more candid conversations.

Reflecting on the Past

Reminding your teen of the times they relied on you when they were younger can also help bridge the gap. Adolescents sometimes forget that you were once their primary source of support and guidance. You might say, "Remember when you used to come to me for help with school projects or when you were scared about starting a new school? I'm still here for you and you can count on me just like you did back then."

This reflection on shared experiences not only evokes nostalgia but also reinforces the idea that your relationship is built on mutual support. You can recall specific moments when they sought your help, illustrating your role as a trusted guide. For example, bringing up a time when they were anxious about a sports event and how you helped them prepare can remind them that you're still their ally.

Emphasizing Your Intentions

It's also helpful to convey to your teen that you genuinely have their best interests at heart. Share with them your desire for their success, whether academically, socially, or personally. You can say, "I want you to succeed in life, and that's why I'm here to listen. I care about your thoughts, feelings, and challenges." By making it clear that your intentions are rooted in love and care, you create an environment where your teen feels safe discussing their triumphs and struggles.

This approach can be particularly effective when your teen faces tough situations, like bullying or academic pressure. Instead of focusing solely on the problem, remind them that your primary goal is to help them tackle these challenges. For instance, if they feel overwhelmed with schoolwork, expressing your understanding can open the door to discussing their feelings about it: "I know school can be stressful. Let's talk about what's been bothering you and see how I can help."

Showing Genuine Interest

To foster a strong line of communication, you must demonstrate a genuine interest in your teen's thoughts, feelings, and challenges. Make it a habit to check in regularly. You can consider asking, "How was your day? Is there anything on your mind that you want to share?" These questions can prompt discussions and show that you care about their daily experiences.

Moreover, when they share their thoughts, they listen actively. Responding with phrases, like "That sounds really challenging" or "I can understand why you feel that way" validates their emotions and encourages them to express themselves further.

Let's consider a situation where your teen feels pressured to conform to their peers. By actively listening and showing empathy, you can guide them through their thoughts: "It's okay to feel that way. Many kids your age feel pressure to fit in. Let's talk about how you can handle those situations without compromising who you are."

Building Confidence Through Dialogue

Encouraging your teen to share their feelings and thoughts also builds their confidence. When they see that you are genuinely interested and supportive, it empowers them to express themselves more freely. Over time, this open communication will help them develop vital life skills, like problem-solving, emotional intelligence, and resilience.

Creating an atmosphere of trust and understanding isn't something that happens overnight. It requires ongoing effort and commitment. However, the rewards are immeasurable. As your teen becomes more comfortable discussing their lives, you'll find that the conversations evolve into deeper discussions about their dreams, ambitions, and even their fears.

Listening Without Judgment

As a parent, you know that communication isn't just about speaking; it's equally about listening. In the fast-paced world of adolescence, your teen will have a lot to say, and you must approach these conversations as a good, nonjudgmental listener. This is more than just a nice-to-have skill; it's the foundation for fostering open and honest dialogue with your child.

The Art of Active Listening

Active listening goes beyond simply hearing the words your teen is saying. It involves being fully present, paying attention, and showing empathy. When your teen opens up about their thoughts or concerns, resist the urge to jump in with your opinions or solutions immediately. Instead, focus on what they're expressing. You can practice this by maintaining eye contact, nodding, and providing verbal affirmations like, "I see," or "That sounds really important."

Imagine your teen confiding in you about feeling overwhelmed with schoolwork and friend drama. Resist the urge to respond with, "You need to manage your time better." Try saying, "I hear you. It sounds like you have a lot on your plate. Want to tell me more about what's going on?" This approach validates their feelings and helps them to share more.

Avoiding Interruptions

One of the most common pitfalls in parent-teen conversations is interrupting. You think you're helping by jumping in with advice or suggestions, but this can often shut down communication. Teens may feel like their voices aren't valued, which can lead to them withholding information in the future.

For example, if your son starts talking about a difficult situation with a friend and you interrupt him by saying, "Well, you should just tell him how you feel," he may feel dismissed. Instead, allow him to express his thoughts completely. Once he's finished, you can then ask, "What do you think you want to say to him?" This not only demonstrates your willingness to listen, but also empowers him to come to his conclusions.

Thanking Them for Their Honesty

Another good aspect of being a good listener is responding positively to your teen's honesty, even when what they share may be difficult to hear. If your daughter confides that she tried something she knows you don't approve of, it's vital not to react with anger or disappointment. Instead, thank her for being honest with you. You might say, "I appreciate you telling me this. It shows a lot of courage to be open about your experiences."

This response creates a safe environment where your teen feels comfortable sharing their thoughts without fear of harsh judgment. By practicing gratitude for their honesty, you are laying the groundwork for deeper conversations and building their trust in you.

The Impact of Nonjudgmental Listening

Nonjudgmental listening can profoundly affect your teen's development. When they feel that they can speak freely about their experiences, good or bad, they are more likely to come to you with concerns or questions in the future. This openness can lead to more honest discussions about challenging topics such as relationships, substance use, or mental health, which can often be difficult for teens to approach.

For instance, if your teen is facing peer pressure to try alcohol at a party, a strong foundation of nonjudgmental communication can make them more likely to come to you for advice rather than hide their struggles. They may say, "I'm feeling pressured to drink at a party this weekend. What should I do?" Your response could guide them without the fear of them feeling judged.

Building Trust Through Consistent Listening

Consistency in your listening approach is required. Make it a habit to be available for your teen, even in small moments. It can be during a quiet drive to school or while you're both preparing dinner together. These small interactions can significantly enhance your relationship, allowing them to feel that they can approach you anytime.

Consider a situation where your teen seems distant or withdrawn. Instead of forcing a conversation, try asking open-ended questions during casual moments: "How do you feel about school this week?" This allows them to share when they're ready rather than feeling pressured to engage in a lengthy discussion.

Acknowledging Their Feelings

When your teen shares something, acknowledge their feelings. Rather than brushing aside their concerns, reflect back on what you hear. For example, if your child expresses anxiety about an upcoming exam, saying, "It sounds like you're really worried about this. It's okay to feel that way," can validate their emotions. This acknowledgment helps your teen feel seen and understood rather than dismissed.

Perhaps you had a passion for sports but faced rejection when trying out for a team. You may share, "I really wanted to be on the soccer team, but I didn't make it my first year. It hurt a lot at the time. However, I learned to keep trying and eventually made the team the following year. That taught me that perseverance is key." By sharing these struggles, you're teaching your teen resilience and the importance of not giving up, even when faced with obstacles.

Bridging the Gap: Sharing Your Own Experiences

As a parent, you may sometimes feel that there's an unbridgeable gap between your teen's world and your own. The truth is that, while the challenges they face may seem unique to their generation, the feelings and struggles of adolescence have remained remarkably consistent over the years. One of the most effective ways to foster communication with your teen is to share your own experiences, struggles, decisions, and even regrets as a teen. This transparency can help create a more profound connection between you and your child.

Assuring Them: "I've Been Where You Are"

When your teen is navigating the turbulent waters of adolescence, reassurance can be invaluable. Let them know, "I've been where you are, and I want to help." By conveying this sentiment, you remind them that they are not alone in their experiences.

For instance, if your daughter is grappling with feelings of inadequacy due to social media comparisons, you might recall your own experiences. You can say, "I remember feeling like I didn't measure up to others when I was your age, especially with everyone posting their highlight reels. It's tough, but it doesn't define your worth." Sharing this sentiment not only validates their feelings but also helps them see that you understand the challenges they face.

Sharing Your Decisions as a Teen

Discussing the decisions you made as a teenager can also be an enlightening experience for your child. When you open up about your choices (both good and bad), it gives them a real-life context for understanding the consequences.

For example, if you were faced with peer pressure to skip school, you can share, "I remember a time when I felt pressured to ditch school with my friends. I thought it would be fun, but I regretted it later when I fell behind in my studies. It's a temptation that can feel overwhelming, but making choices that align with your values is what matters most." This candid approach not only provides insight into the decision-making process, but also encourages your teen to think critically about their own choices.

Discussing Your Struggles and Successes

Adolescence is a time filled with a mix of successes and setbacks. Sharing both aspects of your journey can provide your teen with a more holistic view of growing up. When they see you as a person who has faced difficulties and triumphs, it humanizes your experiences and fosters empathy.

Reflecting on Regrets

Discussing regrets can be one of the most impactful ways to connect with your teen. It's important to approach this topic with care, emphasizing that everyone makes mistakes and that those mistakes can be valuable learning experiences.

If you regret not taking your studies seriously in high school, you might say, "I wish I had focused more on my schoolwork. I didn't realize how important those grades would be for my future. I struggled in college because of it. If I could go back, I would definitely take my studies more seriously." This admission allows your teen to see that they don't have to make the same mistakes you did. It opens the door for conversations about the importance of education and the potential consequences of not prioritizing it.

Timing is key when sharing your experiences. Look for opportunities when your teen seems reflective or open to discussion.

Encouraging Open Dialogue

As you share your own experiences, politely ask your teen to respond. Ask them questions that allow them to express their thoughts and feelings. For example, you might ask, "How do you feel when you're faced with difficult decisions?" or "What do you think about my choices?" This dialogue not only reinforces that you're a trusted confidant but also allows them to process their own feelings in a safe space.

When you create an atmosphere of openness, your teen may be more willing to share their struggles, decisions, and feelings in return. This back-and-forth exchange strengthens your bond and establishes a foundation of trust that can last well beyond adolescence.

By opening the lines of communication, you've taken the first step to connect deeply with your teen. Now, building that foundation of trust is necessary. In the next chapter, we'll focus on how to be trustworthy, which is vital for creating an open and honest relationship with your teen.

Chapter 2: Be Trustworthy

Trust is the bedrock of any relationship, including the one you share with your teen. You can think of it as a delicate bridge that connects you both; it takes time to build and can easily be damaged.

As parents, the goal isn't just to communicate effectively but to create an environment where your teen feels safe to share their thoughts and feelings without fear of judgment or betrayal.

In this chapter, we'll explore the importance of trust and how you can nurture it within your relationship with your teen.

The Foundation of Trust: Truthfulness and Honesty

At the heart of trust lie truthfulness and honesty. Your teen needs to know that you will always tell them the truth, even when it's uncomfortable. Consider a situation in which your teen may have come home from school upset because they overheard gossip about themselves. Instead of minimizing their feelings or offering a cliché response, being honest about the complexities of teenage social dynamics can foster trust.

You can say, "I know it hurts to hear people talk about you like that. When I was your age, I also faced rumors, and it made me feel terrible. But remember, people often talk out of jealousy or misunderstanding. You are so much more than what they say." By validating their feelings and sharing your own experiences, you demonstrate that you're committed to being honest, even when the topic is tough.

Inviting the Conversation: "Do You Trust Me?"

A powerful way to gauge your teen's feelings about trust is to ask them directly. Initiating a conversation about trust can be eye-opening. Ask, "Do you feel like you can trust me? Why or why not?" This question can lead to meaningful dialogue. Your teen may express feelings they've kept bottled up, such as, "Well, sometimes you don't really listen to what I have to say," or, "I don't think you understand what I'm going through."

Listen closely to their responses without becoming defensive. If they mention specific instances that eroded their trust, such as when you accidentally shared something they confided in you, acknowledge their feelings. This opens the door to honest communication, showing them that their thoughts matter to you.

Apologizing When Trust Is Broken

If you've made a mistake that has broken your teen's trust, it's important to acknowledge it and apologize sincerely. For example, if you promised to keep something confidential but inadvertently mentioned it to someone else, let your teen know you recognize the breach.

You might consider saying, "I'm really sorry for sharing what you told me. I didn't mean to betray your trust, and I understand if you're upset with me. I value what you share, and I'll do better in the future." This confession shows humility and reinforces the importance of trust in your relationship. Remember, you are not only saying sorry; you are taking steps to ensure it doesn't happen again.

The Promise of Honesty

Assuring your kids that you will always be honest with them is also helpful in rebuilding or maintaining trust. Establishing that you're committed to transparency in your relationship is important. Consider saying, "I want you to know that I'll always be truthful with you.

It's important that you feel safe coming to me about anything, and I promise to do my best to be honest in our conversations."

This promise sets the stage for open dialogue. Your teen may still be cautious initially, but over time, your consistent honesty can help restore and strengthen their trust in you.

The Impact of Trust on Communication

When your teen trusts you, they are more likely to share their thoughts and feelings openly. This trust creates a safe space for deeper conversations about sensitive topics. If they know they can rely on you to be truthful, they may feel more comfortable discussing issues like peer pressure, mental health, or academic challenges.

Consider the scenario in which your teen feels overwhelmed with school. If they trust you, they will say, "Mom, I'm really stressed about my grades, and I don't know how to handle it." This is an invitation to have a heart-to-heart discussion about what they're experiencing, allowing you to offer support and guidance.

Building Trust Through Consistency

You can build trust by respecting their privacy. If your teen is comfortable sharing personal thoughts or struggles, avoid probing too deeply or sharing their stories with others. Instead, listen, support, and validate their feelings. This respect fosters a stronger bond and deepens their trust in you.

Leading by Example

Always know that your actions speak volumes about the importance of trust. Show trustworthiness not only in your words but also in your behavior. For instance, if your teen confides in you about a friend's struggles, respect their confidentiality. When your teen sees that you honor trust in your relationships, they will feel inspired to do the same.

You can also share stories about your own relationships, like how you navigate trust with friends or family. By being open about your experiences, you model the values of trust and honesty, reinforcing their significance in your teen's life.

Encouraging Honesty Through

Acceptance and Support

Creating an environment where your teen feels comfortable being honest with you starts with acceptance. It's important to understand that when your teen opens up, they take a huge step towards vulnerability. They are sharing parts of themselves that may not always be easy to discuss, and your response can shape their willingness to be honest in the future.

In this part, we will explore how you can encourage honesty through acceptance, commendation, and constructive conversations, even when unexpected revelations arise.

Acceptance: The First Step to Honesty

When your teen shares something that surprises or concerns you, it's vital to approach the conversation with an open mind. Imagine your teen comes to you and admits that they tried vaping at a party. Your initial reaction may be shock or concern, but you will need to resist the urge to condemn them. Instead, focus on accepting their honesty.

You can respond by saying, "I appreciate you telling me about this. It's brave of you to share." This simple acknowledgment can go a long way. When your teen feels accepted, they are more likely to continue sharing openly with you in the future, knowing that their honesty won't lead to immediate punishment or judgment.

Commending Honesty: A Positive Reinforcement

Commending your teen for their honesty is an effective way to reinforce this behavior. When your teen shares their feelings or reveals a mistake, recognize their courage. You can tell them, "Thank you for being honest with me about what happened. I know it wasn't easy to share that with me."

For example, if your teen comes clean about struggling with their grades, acknowledging their honesty shows that you value their willingness to communicate. Saying something like, "I'm glad you told me. It's okay to struggle sometimes; let's figure out how we can tackle this together," opens the door to problem-solving instead of punishment.

Managing Your Reactions: Staying Calm and Collected

It's natural to have strong reactions when your teen reveals something unexpected, but managing those reactions is vital. If your teen admits to sneaking out to go to a party, your instinct may be to react angrily. However, flying off the handle can shut down communication and make your teen feel defensive.

Instead, take a moment to breathe and collect your thoughts. Acknowledge the situation calmly: "I'm surprised to hear that, and I'd like to understand what led you to make that choice." This approach encourages open dialogue and lets your teen explain their reasoning without feeling judged.

Discussing Mistakes: Focus on Solutions, Not Punishment

If your teen has made a mistake, like trying alcohol or lying about their whereabouts, it's a very sensitive situation. Here, you need to pay attention to solutions rather than punishment. While it's natural to feel disappointed, an overly harsh response can lead to resentment and further secrecy. So, approach the situation with a mindset of collaboration.

For instance, if your teen confesses that they drank at a friend's house, you could say, "I appreciate you telling me. Let's talk about how we can prevent situations like this in the future." Discussing the next steps shows your teen that you're invested in their growth and well-being. It also creates a space for them to express their feelings and learn from their experiences.

Navigating Repentance: Acknowledging Feelings of Guilt

When teens admit to making poor choices, they often experience feelings of guilt or regret. Acknowledging these emotions can help them deal with these emotions. If your teen expresses remorse for a mistake, tell them it's okay to feel that way. You can also say, "I can see that you're upset about what happened. It's important to learn from our mistakes."

Encourage your teen to think about how they can make amends or rectify the situation. For example, if they lied about their whereabouts, you might suggest they apologize to the friend they deceived, or if they tried something they regret, talk about how they can make better choices in similar situations in the future.

Collaborating on Solutions: Learning Together

As you discuss the next steps, involve your teen in the conversation. Ask them what they think would be an appropriate way to remedy their mistake. For instance, if they were caught in a lie, ask, "How do you think you can regain trust with me or your friends?" This collaborative approach empowers your teen to take ownership of their actions and promotes accountability.

You can also suggest, "Let's brainstorm ways to avoid situations like this. Would you feel comfortable sharing your plans with me next time?" This will foster responsibility and reinforce that you're in this together. You're not just the enforcer of rules; you're a partner in their growth and decision-making.

Establishing Ground Rules: A Framework for Honesty

Creating clear ground rules can help establish expectations for honesty within your relationship. Discuss what honesty means in your household and why it matters. You can explain, "We value honesty because it helps us trust each other. I want you to feel that you can talk to me about anything without fear."

This conversation can include discussing the consequences of dishonesty as well. When your teen understands the importance of honesty and the potential fallout from lying, they are more likely to approach you with the truth, even when it's difficult.

Creating a Culture of Openness

Ultimately, fostering an environment where your teen feels safe to be honest requires consistent effort. Celebrate the small moments of truth-telling. If your teen shares something minor, like a disagreement with a friend, take the opportunity to commend them for being open. Your encouragement creates a culture of openness in which honesty is valued.

Encourage family discussions where everyone can share thoughts without fear of being condemned. For example, family meetings can serve as a platform for everyone to discuss their week, challenges, and successes. This practice not only strengthens family bonds but also sets an example for your teen regarding the importance of sharing experiences.

Building Trustworthiness: Earning Respect Together

When your teen has demonstrated trustworthiness, it leaves a good memory if you acknowledge and commend them. Recognition plays an important role in reinforcing positive behaviors and encouraging your teen to continue making good choices. You can say something like, "I've noticed how responsible you've been lately, especially with your schoolwork and helping around the house. I'm proud of you!"

Recognizing specific examples of your teen's successes can make your praise even more impactful. For instance, if your teen managed to complete their homework on time without reminders or showed maturity in handling a conflict with a friend, highlight those achievements. "I was impressed when you talked it out with Sam instead of letting it escalate. That shows a lot of maturity." This type of recognition not only boosts their self-esteem but also reinforces their understanding of what trustworthiness looks like.

Addressing Past Honesty Issues: A Constructive Approach

If your teen has struggled with honesty in the past, it's time that you address these issues directly but compassionately. Let them know that everyone makes mistakes and emphasizes the learning opportunities these moments provide. Start by saying something like, "I know there have been times when things weren't as open between us, and that's okay. It happens to all of us."

It's important to outline specific areas where improvements can be made. For example, if your teen has been less than honest about their whereabouts, you can try saying, "I trust you, but you need to understand why being truthful about where you are matters. It helps me know you're safe." This way, you're highlighting the negative behavior and explaining the importance of honesty in maintaining trust simultaneously.

Setting Goals for Improvement: Collaborating on Next Steps

Once you've addressed the past, shift the focus toward the future. Involve your teen in the conversation about how they can improve their trustworthiness moving forward. Ask questions, like, "What do you think you could do differently next time to ensure you're being honest?" This invites them to take ownership of their actions and decisions.

Collaborative goal-setting is a powerful tool. For example, if your teen admits to struggling with being open about their feelings, you can agree on a plan in which they commit to sharing at least one thing about their day during dinner. This promotes regular communication and creates a safe space for them to practice being honest.

Additionally, outline the steps both of you can take to foster a trustworthy environment. You can agree on regular check-ins where you openly discuss challenges or concerns. This mutual commitment reinforces the idea that trust is a two-way street. You can tell them, "Let's make it a habit to check in with each other every Sunday evening. We can talk about our week and anything on our minds."

Building Respect Through Consistency and Reliability

Trustworthiness is often built on a foundation of consistency and reliability. As your teen strides toward being more honest, it's equally important to show respect for their efforts. When they share openly or try to be trustworthy, acknowledge that growth with comments like, "I appreciate you being upfront with me today. It shows you're really trying."

On the flip side, as you work toward improving trust, it's also vital to model trustworthy behavior yourself. Your actions should align with your words. If you promise to be there for them at a specific event or to support them in a challenge, ensure that you follow through. This consistency not only builds your credibility as a parent, but also sets a standard for what trustworthiness looks like.

Encouraging Open Dialogue: The Importance of Mutual Respect

Respect in any relationship goes both ways. As your teen learns to earn your respect through their actions, it's equally important for you to show respect for their autonomy and individuality. This includes valuing their opinions and allowing them to express themselves freely. When they feel respected, they are more likely to reciprocate that respect.

Building a Culture of Trust and Respect

Ultimately, fostering an environment of trust and respect demands ongoing effort from both parents and teens. Establishing family values centered around trustworthiness can help reinforce these principles. For instance, create a family motto that focuses on the importance of honesty and respect, such as "In our family, we trust and support each other."

Consider incorporating trust-building activities into family life. These can involve team-building exercises or discussions about real-life scenarios where trust plays a key role. By engaging in these activities together, you not only strengthen your family bonds, but also create a culture in which trust and respect thrive.

Trust and Freedom: Earning Privileges Together

When your teen values trustworthiness, you can tell them that this behavior can lead to greater freedom and privileges. Allowing them to take on more responsibility can empower them and help them feel valued within the family dynamic. The conversation about privileges should be a collaborative effort, creating a sense of ownership and accountability for your teen.

Engaging Your Teen in the Conversation

Start by asking your teen what specific privileges they are interested in. This can be anything from later curfews, the freedom to use the family car, or the opportunity to attend social events with friends. Phrasing the question openly urges them to express their desires and feel involved in the decision-making process. You can say, "What freedoms do you feel you've earned? Let's talk about how we can make that happen."

For example, if your teen mentions wanting to stay out later on weekends, explore their reasons. *Are they part of a social group that meets regularly? Do they want to attend events that end later?* Understanding their perspective lets you gauge whether their request is reasonable and based on responsibility.

Setting Clear Expectations and Next Steps

Once your teen has shared what privileges they would like to earn, take the steps they need to take to gain those freedoms. This discussion should focus on transparency and mutual understanding. Let them know that earning privileges is a process that mandates a consistent demonstration of trustworthiness.

For instance, if your teen desires to use the family car, outline the conditions they must meet. You should clarify, "If you want to drive the car, you'll need to maintain good grades and keep up with your chores at home. Let's check in each week to see how you're doing." This approach not only sets clear expectations, but also provides a timeline for assessment.

Providing Guidance and Support

While outlining the steps for earning privileges, you will need to offer guidance and support. Let your teen know you're there to help them succeed. You can suggest, "If you're having trouble balancing schoolwork and chores, let's devise a plan together. I'm here to support you."

If your teen struggles with time management, you can introduce them to tools like planners or apps to help them stay organized. Encouraging them to take the initiative in this process can also lead to valuable life skills. For example, you can ask, "Why don't you create a weekly schedule that includes your homework and chores? It'll help you see where you can fit in your social activities, too."

Celebrating Progress and Building Trust

As your teen takes steps toward earning their desired privileges, celebrate their progress. Positive support and rewards can go a long way in motivating them to maintain their trustworthy behavior. Acknowledge when they complete their responsibilities or show maturity in decision-making.

For example, if your teen successfully completes their homework and chores for a month, recognize their efforts by saying, "I'm really proud of how you managed your responsibilities this month. You've shown a lot of growth, and I think you're ready for that later curfew we discussed."

The Balance of Trust and Responsibility

It's important to communicate that trust and responsibility go hand in hand. While you're extending privileges, remind your teen that with increased freedom comes the expectation of accountability. They should understand that trust can be fragile and must be nurtured. Tell them, "Just remember, the more freedoms you have, the more I'll expect you to be responsible. If something happens that shows I can't trust you, we may need to reevaluate.

Trustworthiness is deeply rooted in the ability to keep promises, both big and small. When you make a promise to your teen, whether attending their soccer game or to help them with a project, following through is vital. It shows them that your word holds value and that you respect their time and feelings.

For example, if you tell your teen you'll help them study for an important exam, make it a priority to show up. If something unavoidable arises and you can't be there, communicate that immediately and suggest an alternative time to meet. This transparency reinforces the idea that keeping promises is a two-way street.

Keep Your Promises

Motivate your teen to reflect on their own promises as well. If they agree to take out the trash or complete a homework assignment, underline the importance of following through. When they do keep their promises, acknowledge and celebrate their efforts. Celebrating these moments helps build their understanding of accountability and reinforces a culture of trust within your relationship. By consistently keeping your promises, you establish a strong foundation of reliability, encouraging your teen to do the same.

Establishing a mutual promise of trust between you and your teen can be a transformative step in your relationship. Sit down together and discuss the importance of being completely trustworthy with one another. This open dialogue can help reinforce the idea that trust is a shared responsibility.

You can say something like, "Let's both commit to being honest with each other from now on. I promise to listen to you without judgment, and I'd like you to promise to share your thoughts and feelings honestly." This agreement fosters a sense of security.

Encourage your teen to share their thoughts on what trust means to them. Perhaps they'll express a desire for more privacy or the freedom to make their own decisions. Acknowledge these points and reassure them that their input matters.

Revisit this promise regularly to keep the lines of communication open. Discuss what happened and how you can rebuild trust if trust is broken. By committing to be trustworthy, both you and your teen can cultivate a relationship built on honesty, respect, and understanding, ultimately strengthening your bond.

Start With a Clean Slate

Starting with a clean slate can be a powerful way to revitalize your relationship with your teen. This fresh beginning allows both of you to set aside past misunderstandings and focus on building a more trusting and open connection.

You can also initiate this process by having a candid conversation about your shared goals. For instance, you might say something like, "Let's put any past issues behind us and work on building a better relationship moving forward." This acknowledgment of past challenges can pave the way for more productive dialogue.

Encourage your teen to express any lingering frustrations they may have and be open to listening without becoming defensive.

Together, outline what a clean slate looks like for both of you. This can mean agreeing to communicate more frequently or even setting aside specific times each week to check in with one another. By committing to this new approach, you signal to your teen that you are dedicated to nurturing a more positive and trusting relationship, free from the weight of past grievances.

As we move forward, we'll explore the importance of being reliable. Building trust doesn't stop here. It's reinforced by consistently being there when your teen needs you.

Chapter 3: Be Reliable

Reliability is the next important thing that can help you build trust with your children. It's about showing up physically, emotionally, and mentally when they need you most. As a parent, you already know the worth of reliability in all walks of life, from work to friendships. It is even more crucial to maintain a healthy relationship with your teen. Your reliability becomes the anchor that helps them feel secure, knowing they can count on you no matter what.

However, reliability, just like trust, is a two-way street. Teens have their own expectations of their parents, often unspoken but deeply felt. They may not always voice it, but your consistency and dependability greatly shape their trust. Your teen wants to know that you are there for them; more than that, they need to feel it.

So, let us learn what they expect from you.

Teen's Expectations of Parents

Your teen may expect you to be a safe space—a person they can turn to without fear of judgment or anger. This doesn't mean they always know how to articulate these needs, but they certainly feel them. If you've been consistent in showing up for them by keeping your word or simply being present when they need to talk, they're likely to trust you more.

On the other hand, if there have been times when they felt let down, this may create a sense of uncertainty. Maybe you missed a sports event that was important to them, or perhaps you were too preoccupied with work to notice when they were struggling in school. These moments, while seemingly small, can add up and influence how reliable they perceive you to be.

So, once again, you need to open the conversation by asking your teen directly, "What do you expect from me? Where can I do better?" It's important to remind them that, just like any relationship, there's room for growth on both sides.

What Are Parents Providing Reliably?

As a parent, you're already providing a lot of stability and support, often without even realizing it. You're likely handling their meals, ensuring they have a roof over their heads, and keeping track of their schoolwork and activities. You are reliable in providing a home, food, clothing, transportation, guidance, and love. These day-to-day actions are the backbone of reliability, and even though teens may not always acknowledge them, they count on them deeply.

For instance, your teen knows they can depend on you to drive them to school or pick them up from a friend's house. They also know you'll be there to help them solve a problem or give advice when needed. These are the things they've come to rely on, even if they don't always express it directly.

So, don't be afraid to ask yourself if there are areas where you can offer more emotional reliability. *Are you truly present during conversations, or are you multitasking? Can your teen come to you with personal concerns, or do they feel like they need to figure things out* independently? Ensuring you're physically and emotionally available can make all the difference.

Trust isn't built overnight; it requires consistent effort. You need to make it a point to follow through on your commitments. If you say you'll attend your teen's soccer game, show up. Set aside dedicated time if you promise to help them with a project. These actions demonstrate reliability and reinforce their belief that you can be trusted.

Where Can Parents Improve?

No human being is perfect, and that goes for parents as well. Know that it's okay to not be perfect all the time. The only thing that matters is knowing where you can improve as a reliable figure in your teen's life. It is one of the powerful steps toward strengthening your bond. Ask yourself, *"Am I consistent with my promises?"* You may not notice, but teens quickly notice when you say you'll do something but fail to follow through, even if it's small things like, "We'll talk later" or "I'll help you with that project tomorrow."

If you've let them down in the past, don't be afraid to admit it.

Sometimes, the improvement may also involve creating healthier boundaries. You can realize that you need to better balance work or other commitments with being there for your teen. Or maybe you need to adjust how you respond when they ask for help, ensuring they feel heard and understood.

What Are the Privacy Boundaries Teens Want Respected?

One area where reliability intersects with respect is honoring your teen's privacy. As they grow, their need for personal space and boundaries increases. Part of being reliable is respecting their need for autonomy while still offering guidance and assistance. It's important to have a conversation clearly about what privacy means to them and where the boundaries are.

For example, your teen can feel uncomfortable with you entering their room without knocking, or perhaps they want more control over their social media accounts. These are valid concerns, and as a reliable parent, you should approach them with an open and accepting mind. By respecting their privacy, you're showing that you trust them, which can encourage them to trust you more.

Ask your teen directly: "Are there any boundaries you'd like me to respect regarding your privacy?" This lets them know that their space and opinions matter. At the same time, explain that privacy comes with responsibility. Let them know that while you respect their need for independence, you'll also need to ensure their safety and well-being.

Parent's Expectations of Teens

Now that you have explored what your child expects, let us discuss your expectations. As a parent, it's natural to have certain expectations of your teen, just as they have expectations of you. These guidelines aren't meant to be burdensome, but to help create a sense of responsibility and balance in your household. Teens thrive when they have clear boundaries and understand what is expected of them; while it may not always seem like it, structure gives them a sense of security.

Starting a conversation about expectations can help clarify what both you and your teen need from each other to make day-to-day life smoother. This also allows your teen to voice any concerns or suggest changes, making them feel heard and valued. Open discussions about expectations create a sense of teamwork, which is crucial for maintaining a healthy relationship.

Teens Should Be Forthcoming About Where They Go and With Whom

One of your biggest concerns is probably knowing where your teen is and who they are with. It's not about being nosy or controlling, but about ensuring their safety. By asking your teen to be transparent about their plans, you're setting the expectation that communication is needed, especially when it comes to their whereabouts.

Make sure your teen understands that you're not asking for these details because you don't trust them, but because it's your responsibility as a parent to know they're safe. You can say, "I trust you to make good decisions, but it's important for me to know where you'll be in case anything happens or you need help."

For example, if your teen is going out with friends, ask them to let you know where they're going and who they're with. A quick text message with an update can go a long way in easing your concerns. In return, you can offer to respect their time with friends without constant check-ins or interruptions, reinforcing your trust.

Teens Are Expected to Be Home by Supper Time Each Day

Routine and structure are healthy for teens, even if they resist them. Having a set time for meals, particularly supper, helps ground the family and provides a time to connect. You can use this opportunity to catch up with your teen about their day, share your own experiences, and discuss any issues that may arise.

Let your teen know that being home by supper isn't only about the meal. It is about enjoying family time. By setting this expectation, you establish that these moments together are important and worth prioritizing. It's a chance for everyone to slow down, check in, and be present with each other.

If your teen goes out after school or on the weekends, remind them that they are still expected to be home by supper unless they've made other arrangements with you in advance. Flexibility can be built into this expectation. For example, if they have a special event or activity, they need to let you know ahead of time. But the key is that this time together remains a priority.

Teens Are Expected to Keep Their Room Clean and Neat

A teen's room is their personal space, and they often treat it as a reflection of their personality and mood. However, it's still part of your home, and keeping it clean and tidy is a reasonable expectation. This doesn't mean their room has to look perfect all the time, but maintaining a basic level of cleanliness shows respect for the shared living environment.

When discussing this expectation with your teen, try to find a middle ground. Instead of demanding an immaculate room, you should set certain standards, such as keeping dirty clothes off the floor, trash in the bin, and the bed made. You can say, "I know your room is your space, but keeping it clean is part of living together. It doesn't have to be spotless, but keeping it tidy will make both of us happier."

Make sure to commend your teen when they meet these expectations. Positive reinforcement goes a long way in encouraging good habits. For example, when you see that their room is clean without you having to ask, take a moment to say, "Hey, I noticed you've been keeping your room really neat. I appreciate that."

Teens Are Expected to Complete Their Chores

Chores are also a part of learning responsibility and teamwork. When teens help around the house, they contribute to the family and learn valuable life skills. It's important to have clear expectations about their chores and when they need to be done. For example, if they're responsible for taking out the trash or washing the dishes, set a routine so they know when these tasks need to be completed.

Teens may sometimes forget or delay their chores, especially when focused on schoolwork or social activities. However, reminding them constantly can create friction. Instead, set the expectation that these chores are their responsibility and they need to complete them without being nagged.

One approach is to create a shared calendar or chore chart that everyone in the family follows. This gives your teen a visual reminder of what they need to do and takes the pressure off you to constantly remind them. When your teen consistently completes their chores, be sure to commend them. You can say something like, "Thanks for doing your chores today without me having to remind you. It really helps keep things running smoothly."

If they're falling behind on their responsibilities, approach the conversation calmly and honestly. You can start the conversation by saying, "I noticed you've been putting off your chores lately. Let's talk about what's going on and how we can get back on track." This opens up a dialogue instead of leading with frustration or anger.

Parents Should Discuss Any Other House Rules the Teen Is Expected to Abide By

Every family has its own set of house rules, and these rules must be clear and consistently enforced. Whether it's about curfews, screen time, or how the family handles meals and social time, these expectations should be laid out so your teen understands. House rules shouldn't feel like a list of restrictions; they are guidelines that help the family function smoothly.

Involving your teen in creating or revising house rules can also make them feel more responsible and invested in following them. Ask them what they think about certain rules or if they have suggestions for improving them. For example, if your family has a rule about no phones at the dinner table, you can say, "What do you think about our no-phone rule during meals? Do you think it's fair, and is there a way we can improve it?"

This process fosters respect on both sides and shows that you value their input. At the same time, be clear that some rules are non-negotiable, particularly regarding safety or behavior. You can explain the reasoning behind these rules so your teen understands that they're there for a reason, not just as arbitrary limits.

Know the Parents of Your Teen's Friends

As a parent, getting to know the parents of your teen's friends is an important step in understanding the environment your teen is growing up in. The people your teen interacts with outside of the house, especially their friends and the parents of those friends, can have a significant influence on their behavior, values, and decision-making processes. Engaging with these other parents isn't about controlling your teen's social circle, but rather ensuring that you clearly understand the shared values (or lack thereof) within their extended network.

Do You Share the Same Moral Standards?

Each family has its own set of moral values and standards, particularly when it comes to sensitive subjects such as alcohol, dating, drugs, honesty, and premarital sex. As a parent, you've likely taken the time to instill these values in your teen, setting expectations around behavior and decision-making. When your teen starts spending time at other homes, it's natural to want to know whether the same values are upheld in those environments.

For instance, if your family has clear rules about underage drinking, it's helpful to know if your teen's friend's parents hold similar standards. *Are they strict about not allowing alcohol at home, or are they more lenient, perhaps even allowing their teens to drink in moderation at parties?* A conversation with these parents can reveal how aligned your approaches are and help you determine whether you feel comfortable with your teen spending time in their home.

It's important to approach these conversations delicately. Instead of outright interrogating the other parents, try to frame it as a discussion about mutual understanding. You can say, "We have a pretty firm rule in our home about not allowing our teen to drink, and we're curious what your thoughts are on that topic. It's always helpful to be on the same page when our kids are spending time together."

This same approach can be applied to discussions on topics like dating and drugs. If your family has open conversations about relationships, or if you've set boundaries around dating, knowing if your teen's friend's parents have similar guidelines can provide peace of mind. Maybe they also encourage healthy discussions about relationships or take a different approach. These differences can be important when it comes to understanding what kind of influence those friends might have on your teen.

Do They Instill Their Moral Standards in Their Teens?

It's one thing for parents to have moral standards; it's another to actively instill those values in their teens. Some parents may have strong beliefs but struggle to communicate those values effectively to their children. Others may take a hands-off approach, believing their teen will "figure it out" as they grow.

When you're getting to know the parents of your teen's friends, observe how they engage with their teens. Do they have open conversations about tough topics like honesty, integrity, and responsible choices? Or do they seem more disconnected from their teen's moral development? This can be tricky to gauge without prying, but casual conversations about parenting can often reveal a lot. For example, you could ask, "How do you approach conversations about honesty with your teen? It's something we've been focusing on lately in our home."

If the other parents are actively working to instill strong moral values in their teen, it can reassure you that your teen is spending time in an environment that reinforces the same principles you've been teaching at home. On the other hand, if you sense a disconnect between their beliefs and their actions, it might give you reason to be more cautious.

Do They Have Meaningful Conversations With Their Teens?

One of the hallmarks of healthy parent-teen relationships is the ability to have meaningful and open conversations. If your teen's friend's parents regularly discuss life, challenges, and personal growth with their children, their home likely fosters a supportive and communicative environment.

Parents who prioritize talking with their teens often create a space where their children feel comfortable coming to them with problems or concerns. This kind of home atmosphere can have a positive ripple effect on your teen. If your teen spends time in a home where open dialogue is encouraged, they may feel supported and safe, even when you're not around. It's reassuring to know that other parents are also invested in helping their teens navigate the challenges of growing up.

When you talk to other parents, it's perfectly normal to ask how they approach tough topics or what their family dynamics are like. You can bring it up casually, saying, "We've been trying to have more open conversations with our teen about school and friends—

how do you handle those kinds of talks in your home?" These conversations provide insight into the role other parents play in their teen's lives and whether they encourage meaningful communication.

Do They Allow Their Teen Privileges and Freedoms That You Do Not?

Teens crave independence, and it's natural for them to want the same privileges as their peers. However, every family has different boundaries regarding freedom. One family may have strict curfews and limitations on screen time, while another may allow their teen to stay out late or spend hours gaming. It's important to know whether the privileges extended to your teen's friends align with what you're comfortable with, especially when your teen starts asking for the same freedoms.

For example, if your teen's friend is allowed to attend unsupervised parties or drive long distances alone, your teen may want to do the same. If you're not comfortable with those privileges, it's worth discussing this with the other parents to understand their reasoning. You can say, "We've been having a conversation about curfews lately, and I'm curious what your approach is. We've been pretty strict about it, but I'd love to hear how you handle it with your teen."

Sometimes, simply understanding another parent's reasoning can help you adjust your own approach or reaffirm your boundaries. At the same time, these discussions can help you prepare for any challenges that might arise when your teen inevitably asks for more freedom.

What Sort of Example Are They Setting for Their Teen?

Parents are role models for their children, whether they realize it or not. Teens absorb behaviors from the adults around them, so it's pivotal to understand what kind of example your teen's friends parents are setting. *Are they modeling healthy habits, such as open communication, respect, and responsibility? Or are they engaging in behaviors that contradict the values you've been trying to instill in your teen?*

For instance, if the other parents smoke, drink excessively, or engage in behaviors that you wouldn't want your teen to mimic, it's important to take note of that. While you can't control what happens in other homes, being aware of the environment can help you have proactive conversations with your teen. You can discuss, "I know that some of your friends' parents have different habits than we do, like smoking or drinking. Let's talk about how that makes you feel and what your thoughts are on those behaviors."

It's not about passing judgment on other parents, but rather being mindful of the influences around your teen. By discussing these behaviors openly with your teen, you can reinforce the values that are important in your own home.

Simply put, reliability builds a stable environment for your teens, where they know they can depend on you. Next, we'll discuss the topic of alcohol, an issue many teens encounter early on. Your reliability will play a big part in guiding them through these challenging situations.

Chapter 4: Alcohol

Introducing alcohol into any conversation with your teen can feel daunting. After all, it's a topic that comes with societal expectations, peer pressure, and even the potential for serious consequences. Yet, it's a conversation that can't be avoided. Teens are often exposed to alcohol long before they reach the legal drinking age, whether through friends, parties, or media portrayals of alcohol as a necessary part of having a good time. As a parent, the example you set regarding alcohol consumption will likely have a lasting impact on your teen's perception of it.

But how can you be sure you're setting the right example? How do you balance this with creating an open environment where your teen feels comfortable discussing alcohol with you?

Let's dive into the complex relationship between parents, teens, and alcohol, starting with an honest reflection on your own behavior and the messages you may be sending without even realizing it.

Do You Drink to Excess or to the Point of Getting Drunk?

One of the most significant ways you can influence your teen's attitude toward alcohol is through your own drinking habits. If you regularly drink excessively—whether that means binge drinking at social gatherings or consuming alcohol frequently—this can send a message to your teen that such behavior is normal or even acceptable.

Let's say, for instance, your teen watches you come home after a long week at work and down several drinks to unwind. They may start to associate alcohol with stress relief or see heavy drinking as a way to cope with life's pressures. The truth is that teens are often looking for ways to deal with the challenges they face in their own lives. If they see a parent turning to alcohol to handle stress, they may follow suit, thinking it's a natural solution.

This is why it's crucial to reflect on your own drinking habits. *Are you setting the kind of example you want your teen to emulate?* If you find that you've been drinking to excess, it's important to acknowledge that behavior, not just to yourself, but also to your teen. It's okay to admit when you've made mistakes or engaged in unhealthy habits. In fact, showing that you can recognize and correct your behavior is an even more powerful lesson for your teen.

Do You Indulge in Alcohol Every Day?

Another key aspect to consider is the frequency of your alcohol consumption. Drinking in moderation may not be inherently harmful; however, when alcohol becomes a daily fixture in your life, it can set the expectation that alcohol is a necessary part of your daily routine. Your kids often mimic your parents' behavior, and if they see you indulging in alcohol every day, they may begin to view it as a normal part of adult life.

For example, suppose your family dinners regularly include a glass of wine or a cocktail. In that case, your teen will start to believe that alcohol is an essential part of socializing or relaxing. This can create a sense of normalization around drinking that may lead to earlier experimentation on their part.

If you find that alcohol has become a daily habit, it might be worth reassessing whether this is the example you want to set. Perhaps cutting back or choosing not to drink during family meals can demonstrate to your teen that alcohol doesn't need to be an everyday occurrence.

Do You Always Serve Alcohol to Your Adult Guests?

Social gatherings can often revolve around alcohol, and it's common for adults to serve drinks when entertaining guests. However, if every social occasion in your home centers around alcohol, it may send the message to your teen that alcohol is necessary for having fun or connecting with others. This can be especially impactful if your teen consistently sees you offering alcohol to your guests, regardless of the occasion.

For instance, consider a family barbecue where adults casually drink beer or wine throughout the day. Your teen may observe how the adults are engaging with each other and having fun, and they may conclude that alcohol is a vital part of the experience. While there's nothing wrong with enjoying a drink, it's worth reflecting on the larger message your teen might be receiving.

Do You Need to Make Changes to Improve the Example You Are Setting?

If you've reflected on your habits and realized that you may be setting an example that could lead to unhealthy behaviors in your teen, don't panic. The fact that you're recognizing this is already a step in the right direction. Being willing to make changes in your own life not only improves your health and well-being, but also shows your teen that it's never too late to adopt healthier habits.

For example, if you've been drinking too much or too frequently, consider cutting back and having an open conversation with your teen about why you're making this change. You can say, "I've noticed that I've been drinking more than I should, and I want to set a better example for you. So, I'm going to work on drinking less and focusing on healthier ways to manage stress." This kind of honesty shows your teen that everyone can make mistakes and that it's important to recognize when change is necessary.

Managing Alcohol in the Home: Setting Boundaries and Trusting Your Teen

One of the more practical considerations regarding parenting and alcohol is whether you choose to keep it in your home. Alcohol is a common presence in many households, but as your teens grow older, the need arises to reassess how accessible that alcohol is. While some teens may respect boundaries, others find the temptation difficult to resist. As a parent, you are responsible for making decisions that best support your teen's ability to make safe, informed choices.

Is Alcohol a Temptation for Your Teen?

It's natural for teens to be curious about alcohol, especially if they see it in the home regularly. They may wonder what it tastes like or feel pressure from peers to experiment. If you have alcohol in the house, it's important to be aware of how your teen feels about it. Some teens may not be particularly interested in trying alcohol, while others may be tempted, especially if they see it as something "forbidden."

For example, imagine you keep a few bottles of wine or beer in the fridge for family gatherings or dinner parties. If your teen has seen you drink responsibly and you've had conversations about the risks of underage drinking, they may not feel tempted to try it. However, for a teen who is more susceptible to peer pressure or who hasn't yet had these discussions with you, the presence of alcohol could feel like a silent invitation to experiment.

It's important to open up a dialogue with your teen. Ask them how they feel about alcohol in the home and whether they feel any pressure (internal or external) to try it. This conversation can provide valuable insight into whether having alcohol in the house might pose a risk.

Taking Precautions: Locking Alcohol Away or Removing It

If you sense that your teen is tempted by the alcohol in your home or if there's any doubt about whether they can resist the urge to experiment, you will need to take preventative measures. One option is to lock the alcohol away. By doing so, you create a clear boundary: alcohol is not for them, and it's kept in a secure place where it won't be easily accessible.

Another option, if you feel the situation calls for it, is to remove alcohol from your home altogether. Although this may seem like a drastic step, if you have concerns about your teen sneaking alcohol or feeling overly tempted, it can be the best way to prevent potential problems.

Commending Responsible Behavior

On the other hand, if you believe your teen can be trusted not to indulge in alcohol without permission, it's important to commend them for their responsible behavior. Trust is a two-way street; when your teen demonstrates that they can handle responsibility, it's essential to recognize and reinforce that.

For example, if your teen has shown maturity by adhering to house rules regarding alcohol or being open and honest about their feelings toward it, let them know you appreciate their honesty and respect for the rules. This builds their confidence and strengthens the trust between you.

Alcohol: Understanding the Risks and Talking With Your Teen

In all countries, there are legal restrictions on the age at which someone can buy and consume alcohol. As a parent, it's vital that you and your teen agree to abide by the laws of your country when it comes to alcohol consumption. Even though your teen may be curious about alcohol, underage drinking is illegal and can lead to serious consequences.

Binge drinking, especially among young people, can be lethal, leading to alcohol poisoning, risky behavior, or even death (Courtney & Polich, 2009). Understanding the risks and creating a space for open dialogue is key to helping your teen make informed choices.

Explaining the Dangers of Alcohol to Your Teen

It's easy for teens to feel invincible, especially when peer pressure is involved. They may think, "One drink won't hurt," or they might not fully understand the consequences of binge drinking. Parents need to clearly explain the short- and long-term effects that alcohol can have on a teen's physical and mental health. They should use examples that teens can relate to and should not shy away from discussing how alcohol affects brain development, impairs judgment, and increases the risk of accidents and injuries.

For instance, you can explain: "I know you've heard about alcohol before, but did you know that it can affect your brain and body differently at your age than it does for adults? When you drink alcohol, it doesn't just impair your judgment; it can also cause long-term damage to your developing brain. That's why it's especially dangerous for teens to drink. When people binge drink, the effects are even more serious—sometimes it can even be fatal."

By framing the conversation regarding health and safety, you create a strong foundation for discussing why it's important to avoid alcohol or, at the very least, to approach it with extreme caution.

Discussing Alcohol Use Among Your Teen's Friends

Once you've explained the risks of alcohol, it's important to move the conversation toward understanding your teen's social environment. Ask them if any of their friends or peers drink alcohol. This isn't about being invasive, but about understanding the pressures they may face when they are with friends. Teens often want to fit in with their peers, and they might feel pressure to drink alcohol to be accepted.

You can also ask, "Have you ever been in a situation where your friends were drinking? How did you feel about it?" This question is open-ended and non-judgmental, which can encourage your teen to be honest. The goal here is to learn about their experiences and how they feel when alcohol is present, rather than making them feel defensive.

If your teen confirms that their friends do drink, you can follow up by discussing how they handled the situation. Ask them how they felt in that moment, whether they felt pressure to join in, and how they responded. This can help you gauge your teen's level of confidence and resilience when it comes to resisting peer pressure.

Addressing Peer Pressure: How Did It Make You Feel?

If your teen shares that they've been pressured to drink by their friends, it's time to explore how that experience made them feel. Ask them directly, "How did you feel when your friend pressured you to drink?" This question helps your teen reflect on their emotions and think critically about the situation.

For example, your teen might say, "I felt uncomfortable, but I didn't want to seem uncool." This is a valuable opportunity for you to acknowledge their feelings while also reinforcing that it's okay to stand up for themselves. You might say, "I understand how hard it can be to say no, especially when you're worried about how it'll look. But your health and safety are more important than what anyone thinks at that moment."

Talking through these emotions helps your teen recognize that their feelings matter and that they have the right to make choices that are best for them, even when it's difficult. This is also a good time to talk about ways they can remove themselves from situations in which they feel uncomfortable.

Evaluating Friendships: Are They a Good Influence?

Peer pressure to drink can be a sign that a friendship may not be as healthy as it seems. After discussing your teen's feelings about being pressured to drink, it's important to help them evaluate that friendship. You can ask them, "How do you feel about the friend who pressured you? Are you close with them? Do you think they're a good influence on you?"

This conversation can help your teen start thinking critically about the relationships in their life. It encourages them to reflect on whether they feel supported by their friends or whether they're being pushed into situations that make them uncomfortable. It's a fine balance for parents to strike; you want to guide your teen without coming across as too judgmental of their friends.

For instance, if your teen expresses doubts about the friendship, you should say, "It's good that you're thinking about whether this person is a positive influence. Not all friendships are forever, and it's okay to distance yourself from people who don't respect your choices."

Preparing for Future Scenarios: What If It Happens Again?

It's also helpful to prepare your teen for future situations. If they've been pressured to drink once, it's likely to happen again. Ask them how they plan to handle it if they find themselves in the same situation in the future. This encourages your teen to think proactively and develop strategies for saying no.

You can ask, "What will you do if it happens again? How do you think you can handle it next time?" Your teen might not have a clear answer right away, but this is an opportunity for you to help them come up with practical ways to deal with peer pressure. For example, they could come up with a polite but firm response like, "No thanks, I'm good," or they could use an excuse, like needing to stay sharp for an early activity the next day.

Open Conversations About Alcohol Use

When you have an open and honest discussion about alcohol, you not only show your concern but also create a safe space for your teen to be truthful. Whether the answer is yes or no, how you respond is essential in reinforcing trust and guiding them in making healthy decisions.

Commend Your Teen for Their Honesty

If your teen admits to having consumed alcohol, the first thing you should do is commend them for their honesty. It's not easy for teens to admit when they've done something they know you might disapprove of. By recognizing their honesty, you reinforce the importance of open communication in your relationship. For example, you can tell them, "I really appreciate your honesty. It takes a lot of courage to share something like that, and it means a lot that you trust me enough to tell me." This acknowledgment strengthens your bond and encourages your teen to come to you in the future with other issues.

Addressing a Potential Alcohol Problem

After thanking your teen for their honesty, ask them if they feel they have a problem with alcohol. Teenagers are often still developing their understanding of boundaries and moderation, and some may not fully realize when their drinking has become an issue. You can gently ask, "Do you feel like drinking is something you struggle with or do too often?" This question allows your teen to reflect on their behavior without feeling judged.

If your teen admits that they feel alcohol has become a problem, it's vital to approach the situation with care and understanding. Instead of responding with anger or disappointment, assure your teen that this is something that can be addressed and that they are not alone in facing it. Let them know that professional help, such as seeing a doctor or therapist, can be an effective way to help them wean off alcohol safely and responsibly. For example, you might consider saying something like, "If you feel like it's become something you can't control, we can talk to a doctor together. What's important is that you know I'm here to support you, no matter what." By offering your help, you show your teen that they are not defined by their struggles. Moreover, you can help them reduce any feelings of shame they might have.

Reassure Your Teen of Your Love and Support

Whether or not your teen struggles with alcohol, one message that should always come across is your unconditional love and support. If your teen admits to drinking, let them know that your love for them hasn't changed and that you will be there to help them through any challenges they face. You can say, "No matter what, I love you, and I'm here for you. We'll figure this out together." This reassurance is critical, reminding your teen that they can rely on you for guidance and support.

Commending Self-Control

If your teen reveals that they have never engaged in drinking alcohol, commend them for their self-control. In today's world, where peer pressure is strong, it's a great accomplishment for a teen to resist it. You must say something like, "I'm really proud of you for making that choice. It shows a lot of strength and maturity." Praising their ability to stand by their values, even when others may not, strengthens the importance of self-discipline and responsible decision-making.

Allowing Controlled Exposure to Alcohol at Home

It's also important to acknowledge that curiosity about alcohol is a natural part of growing up. If you feel that your teen is mature enough and you believe it's the right approach, you may consider allowing them to taste alcohol in the safety of your home, under your supervision. This can help demystify alcohol and make it less of a "forbidden fruit" that they feel compelled to sneak behind your back. That said, if you do decide to allow your teen to try alcohol, it's important to establish clear boundaries and engage in open discussions about responsible consumption.

For example, when teens taste alcohol at home, they are more likely to recognize its taste and effects, which allows them to make informed decisions when they encounter it outside the home. You need to explain to your teen, "I'm allowing you to try this so that if someone offers you a drink when I'm not there, you'll know what it is and how it makes you feel. But this doesn't mean you have my permission to drink with your friends."

Likewise, you need to talk about the potential threats. Discuss the dangers of binge drinking and the long-term effects that alcohol can have on their health, including its potential to cause acne, premature aging, weight gain, and dependency. Explain the risks of chronic alcohol use, such as damage to the liver, heart, and nervous system (Courtney & Polich, 2009). The goal is to make sure your teen understands that alcohol, while legal for adults, is a substance that must be approached with caution and responsibility.

Helping Teens Resist Peer Pressure

Allowing your teen to taste alcohol at home can provide them with a sense of empowerment when faced with peer pressure. If they've already tried alcohol in a safe environment, they may feel more confident in telling their friends, "I've already tried it at home, and I'm not interested in drinking right now." This approach can equip your teen with the tools to resist peer pressure while also maintaining their social standing. It shows that they've had the experience but made a personal choice not to engage in drinking in a risky or unsupervised manner.

Setting Clear Boundaries

It's important, however, to make it clear that allowing them to taste the alcohol at home does not permit them to drink with their friends. Boundaries must be set, and your teen should understand the difference between a supervised experience and unsupervised drinking. You could explain to them, "This isn't a pass for you to start drinking with your friends. This is a way for you to know what it's like in a safe environment so that you can make responsible decisions in the future."

By allowing controlled exposure to alcohol under supervision, you help guide your teen toward responsible behavior while also giving them the tools they need to navigate peer pressure and social situations.

Discussing Consequences for

Unauthorized Alcohol Consumption

Parents and teens must have a clear and open discussion about the consequences of consuming alcohol without permission. Setting these boundaries beforehand helps teens understand the seriousness of the issue and the trust that's at stake. You can explain to your teen that, while they may feel tempted or pressured to drink, there will be repercussions if they do so without parental approval.

For instance, you can tell your teen, "If you choose to drink without our consent, there will be consequences, such as losing privileges like going out with friends or access to your phone." This ensures that your teen is aware of the rules and the potential outcomes of breaking them.

At the same time, be sure to emphasize that the goal of these consequences isn't to punish but to reinforce trust and ensure their safety. You must say, "We're not trying to control you, but we need to be able to trust you. These consequences are meant to help you understand that your actions have real-life implications."

Having this conversation in a calm and understanding manner ensures that your teen knows the expectations and can make more informed choices about their behavior. Now, let's discuss dating, a topic full of questions and emotions. Preparing for these discussions will help you support your teen as they navigate relationships responsibly.

Chapter 5: Dating

Dating is the primary way, in Western culture, that people assess members of the opposite sex as potential marriage mates (Smith, 2023). Unfortunately, teens often engage in dating when they are nowhere near ready for marriage. It is important for you as parents to appreciate that dating is not just a recreational pursuit; it's primarily for adults to assess the suitability of potential marriage mates. It is not an appropriate pastime for teens.

You can start by understanding how much immense pressure your teens are under to date. In today's world, the idea of dating is not just about forming romantic connections; it's also a social milestone that many teens feel obligated to reach to fit in with their peers. If a teen is not dating, they may feel left out or different. It also leads to insecurity or a sense of isolation. They may even face teasing or assumptions from their peers, such as being labeled as *weird* or *uncool*.

It's not uncommon for teens who don't date to be subject to rumors or accusations, such as being called a homosexual, simply because they aren't engaging in relationships like others. While this is completely unfair, it shows just how intense the pressure to conform can be. As a parent, recognizing these challenges can help you approach the subject with greater empathy and support.

This chapter is dedicated to learning all about the dating aspect of your teens.

The Influence of Hormones

Adding to this social pressure is the undeniable surge of hormones that teens experience during puberty. These biological changes naturally make receiving attention from the opposite sex more appealing, and the curiosity about romantic and physical relationships is heightened. Hormonal shifts can create strong emotions and desires, making teens more prone to wanting to explore dating relationships (Hegde et al., 2022).

When these emotions are combined with the peer pressure to date, teens can find themselves feeling conflicted, unsure of what they actually want versus what they believe is expected of them. This is where parental guidance becomes necessary. They need an anchor to help them deal with these stormy waters, and as a parent, you can provide that stability by helping your teen process these feelings and pressures in a healthy way.

Offering Guidance and Support

One of the best things you can do as a parent is to offer open and honest communication about dating and relationships. Teens need to feel safe discussing their thoughts and feelings with you without fear of judgment or punishment. By being approachable, you can create a relationship in which your teen feels comfortable seeking advice when they are unsure about what to do. This can be particularly helpful if they are feeling pressured to date when they aren't emotionally ready.

You can explain that it's perfectly okay not to date just because their friends are doing so. Encourage them to take their time and enter into relationships only when they feel ready, not when others tell them they should. It's also important to convey that dating is not a requirement for social acceptance and that there is strength in standing by their own values and readiness.

Taking Dating Off the Table

Despite the enormous pressure to date, many teens may actually realize deep down that they aren't ready for a romantic relationship. They may not know how to communicate this or fear social consequences. As a parent, you can ease this burden by taking dating off the table for the time being. Doing so gives your teen an excuse to avoid dating without feeling like they are missing out or disappointing anyone.

While the pressure to date can be intense, some teens will realize they aren't ready to take that step. They may feel relieved when their parents step in and set boundaries. You can encourage your teen to take their time, assuring them that dating is not a race and that it's okay to wait until they feel more mature and ready to handle the responsibilities of a relationship. You can also suggest alternatives, such as group outings or activities that don't revolve around dating but still allow for social interaction. This way, your teen can enjoy time with friends without the added pressure of romance.

The Benefits of Group Activities Over One-on-One Dating

As a parent, one of the best ways to guide your teen through the challenges of adolescence, especially regarding relationships, is to encourage group activities rather than dating a single steady person. Group activities provide a healthy, fun, and social environment where teens can build friendships, develop social skills, and experience connections without the pressure of a romantic relationship. This approach allows teens to engage with others in a more relaxed setting, reducing the likelihood of feeling overwhelmed by the emotional and physical complexities that often come with one-on-one dating.

The Safety in Numbers

There's an old saying that rings true when it comes to teens and social interactions: "There is safety in numbers." Encouraging your teen to participate in group outings, whether going to a movie, participating in sports, or attending school events, can lower the chances of them feeling the pressure to pair off romantically. In a group setting, teens are less likely to engage in risky behaviors, such as premarital sex or experimentation with alcohol or drugs, which can sometimes occur when a couple is left alone.

Group activities also give structure and a sense of accountability. With friends around, teens will focus on the shared activity, making it easier to ignore the complications of dating too early. These environments also allow them to observe how others behave and interact, learning valuable lessons about friendships, boundaries, and mutual respect, all without the emotional intensity that can come from exclusive relationships.

Setting Boundaries and Protecting Your Teen

As important as it is for teens to develop independence, this is an area where parents need to assert their authority, especially for teens who are 17 years old or younger. Dating at a young age can often lead to situations that teens are not emotionally or mentally prepared for. This is where your role as a parent becomes vital. By setting clear boundaries around dating, you protect your teen from making decisions they may not fully understand or be ready to handle.

Teens may not always appreciate or agree with the boundaries you set, but they often recognize, later on, the wisdom in your decisions. By encouraging group activities, you are providing a balanced approach that allows them to enjoy socializing and making connections while minimizing the risks associated with early dating. It's not about denying your teen experiences but guiding them through those experiences with a safety net.

Aiding Emotional Development

Another benefit of group activities is that they become a social space for teens to grow emotionally. Teens can develop important life skills in a group setting, such as cooperation, communication, and conflict resolution.

They learn how to relate to others in various contexts without the added pressure of maintaining a romantic relationship. Group dynamics offer valuable lessons in empathy, teamwork, and understanding diverse perspectives.

By contrast, when teens focus on dating one steady person, they may become emotionally wrapped up in that relationship, sometimes to the disadvantage of other friendships or personal growth. Group activities prevent this tunnel vision and encourage your teen to maintain a well-rounded social life.

Long-Term Benefits

When teens are encouraged to participate in group activities rather than dating one steady person, they are more likely to make well-rounded, thoughtful decisions when they eventually begin dating more seriously. These group experiences build the foundation for healthy relationships later on by teaching them how to respect boundaries, communicate effectively, and value friendships. Allowing them to mature emotionally in a group setting gives them the tools to navigate future romantic relationships in a balanced and thoughtful way.

For example, a teen who spends time with a group of friends may develop a strong sense of self-worth and independence, which can stop them from entering unhealthy or codependent relationships later. They will also be able to observe different types of friendships and relationships, gaining insights into what works and what doesn't. This experience can help them when they eventually decide to date.

Early Awareness and the Reality of Premarital Sex

As a parent, you need to be aware that children as young as eleven and twelve years old are engaging in premarital sex in some places. This fact may be uncomfortable, but it reflects the reality that teens are exposed to a variety of influences from social media, peers, and their environment that often push them toward experimenting with intimate relationships at a younger age than you might expect. In some countries, laws even allow teens to access birth control without parental consent, which can further complicate a parent's ability to guide their child through these significant life decisions.

Given this context, you need to take a proactive role in discussing these topics with your teens. Rather than assuming that governmental authorities, schools, or even cultural norms will adequately protect your teen from the potential pitfalls of early sexual activity, you should embrace the responsibility of educating and guiding your children through this challenging stage of development.

Addressing the Temptations and Pressures

Teens today face enormous temptations and pressures when it comes to dating and sexuality. From television and movies to peer pressure, constant messages are telling them that relationships and even sex are a normal part of growing up. Sometimes, they are emotionally or physically ready to handle the consequences. As a parent, one of your most important roles is to explain the real dangers and challenges that come with dating before they are ready for a serious commitment like marriage.

Open and honest discussions about these temptations can help teens understand that not everyone is engaging in activities that might seem "normal" from their point of view. Suppose your teen feels pressured to have a romantic relationship because their friends are dating. In that case, you will need to help them see that waiting until they are emotionally and mentally ready is a valid and responsible choice. Furthermore, you must explain that while dating can seem exciting, it often comes with emotional challenges that can be overwhelming for someone not ready to handle those complexities.

Real-Life Conversations With Your Teen

Instead of simply warning them against dating or issuing blanket rules, you can try reasoning with your teen about the natural desires and temptations they will likely experience.

For example, ask them about their feelings: Are they interested in dating, or do they feel pressured because their friends are? Explain to them that while it's normal to have crushes or feelings of attraction, acting on those feelings too early can lead to situations they may not be ready for emotionally or physically.

Share real-life examples where possible. For instance, if you know of a story where a young person faced challenges because they engaged in a relationship prematurely, share it with your teen. Talk about the emotional toll, possible regrets, and how those involved wished they had waited until they were older and more prepared for such relationships.

Guiding Toward Long-Term Perspective

Ultimately, as a parent, your goal should be to help your teen see the long-term perspective. Dating and romantic relationships should be considered carefully, especially at a young age, because of the potential emotional impacts. Encourage your teen to focus on developing friendships and self-awareness before diving into the complexities of romantic relationships.

By having these conversations early, you give your teen the tools they need to navigate the pressures and temptations they will inevitably face. This way, they can make informed, thoughtful decisions that will set them up for healthier and more successful relationships in the future.

The next chapter, which focuses on drugs, addresses another sensitive topic where teens need your guidance and understanding to stay safe.

Chapter 6: Drugs

Navigating the landscape of teenage life can be challenging, particularly when it comes to the subject of drugs. With peer pressure, curiosity, and the allure of experimentation lurking around every corner, parents need to have open and honest conversations with their teens about the dangers of drug use.

This chapter aims to equip you with the knowledge and strategies needed to address this sensitive topic effectively. By understanding the risks and establishing a supportive dialogue, you can help your teen make informed choices and empower them to resist the temptations that drugs may present.

Understanding Local Drug Availability and Dangers

First things first, you need to be aware of the types of drugs that may be readily available in your local area. Unfortunately, drugs can find their way into schools, neighborhoods, and social circles, putting your teens at risk. Keeping informed about the drug landscape around you can help you be better prepared to have necessary conversations with your teen about the dangers of substance use and how to avoid it.

One of the best resources for understanding which drugs are prevalent in your community is local law enforcement. Police departments often conduct community outreach programs and offer resources to educate parents about the types of drugs circulating in the area, as well as their street names and warning the signs of drug use. You can contact your local police department directly to inquire about drug awareness programs or attend community meetings where law enforcement officers discuss local crime, including drug-related issues.

How to Get Information About Drugs in Your Area

To get accurate and up-to-date information on local drug activity, you can take several steps:

1. **Attend community meetings:** Many neighborhoods and townships host regular community meetings that include updates from local law enforcement. These meetings often address concerns, such as drug activity, including which drugs are being trafficked in the area.

2. **Visit police department websites:** Many police departments now provide online

resources for parents and community members. These resources often include lists of commonly abused drugs, their street names, and signs to look for if you suspect someone is using drugs.

3. **Contact drug prevention programs:** Reach out to local drug prevention programs, which are often run by schools or health departments. They may offer seminars or pamphlets detailing the local drug scene, including common drugs and their side effects.

4. **Use anonymous tip lines:** If you have concerns about drug activity in your area, you can contact anonymous tip lines run by law enforcement to get information or report any suspicions you may have.

Common Street Names and Symptoms of Drugs

Many drugs go by different street names, which makes it harder to recognize if your teen or someone around them is engaging in drug use. Familiarizing yourself with these terms can help you pick up on potential red flags in conversation or behavior changes.

- **Marijuana:** Commonly referred to as "weed," "pot," "bud," or "grass," symptoms of use include bloodshot eyes, increased appetite, dry mouth, and impaired coordination (RN, 2024).

- **Cocaine:** It is often called "blow," "coke," or "snow" symptoms include dilated pupils, restlessness, fast speech, and heightened energy, followed by extreme fatigue.

- **Heroin:** It goes by "smack," "junk," or "dope" signs of heroin use can include lethargy, shallow breathing, constricted pupils, and needle marks on the skin.

- **MDMA (Ecstasy/Molly):** It is known as "E," "X," or "Molly," symptoms include excessive energy, enhanced sensory perception, euphoria, teeth grinding, and dehydration (RN, 2024).

- **Methamphetamine:** Its street names are "crystal," "meth," "ice," or "crank," symptoms include rapid weight loss, hyperactivity, erratic behavior, and skin sores.

- **Prescription Pills (Opioids):** These can go by names like "Percs" (Percocet), "Vikes" (Vicodin), or "Oxy" (OxyContin). Signs to look out for include drowsiness, confusion, constricted pupils, or unexplained pill bottles (RN, 2024).

Recognizing Symptoms of Drug Use

Each drug comes with its own set of physical and behavioral symptoms. However, general warning signs that a teen may be experimenting with drugs include changes in behavior, mood swings, secretive behavior, a sudden drop in academic performance, neglect of personal hygiene, and withdrawal from friends or family.

If you notice any of these changes or suspect that your teen may be using drugs, you need to address the issue calmly, immediately, and without judgment. Open a dialogue and let your teen know that your priority is their safety. If you suspect drug abuse, it may also be necessary to seek professional help or treatment.

Educating Teens on the Dangers of Experimenting With Drugs

As a parent, one of the most important conversations you can have with your teen is about the dangers of experimenting with drugs. The teenage years are often filled with curiosity, peer pressure, and a desire to fit in, so make it a priority to step in and provide clear guidance. They need to understand that experimenting with drugs, even "just once," can lead to a lifetime of consequences that are not only physical but also emotional, legal, and social.

Teens may be exposed to marijuana, cocaine, crack cocaine, heroin, GHB, ecstasy, methamphetamine (meth), hallucinogens, inhalants, opioids, amphetamines, barbiturates, and prescription drugs when dispensed without a prescription. Often these drugs are cut and contaminated with dangerous substances that can be poisonous, even lethal, when ingested. Teens need to be made aware of how dangerous even occasional experimentation can be.

Explaining the Immediate Risks

When discussing drug use with your teen, it's important to highlight the immediate dangers. Experimenting with drugs—whether marijuana, prescription pills, or more dangerous substances like meth or heroin—can have severe short-term effects on the body and mind. These effects can include impaired judgment, coordination issues, and changes in mood or behavior that may lead to accidents or risky decisions. For instance, you can explain that a teen experimenting with drugs at a party may makes the dangerous decision to drive under the influence, putting their life and the lives of others at risk.

Help your teen understand that even substances that may seem harmless, like marijuana or alcohol, can impair their ability to make sound decisions. This can make them vulnerable to physical harm or dangerous situations, such as unprotected sex or violence. By emphasizing the immediate risks, you help ground the conversation in real-life consequences.

You can give clear statistics to help them understand the effects of drug use. According to research conducted in 2023, 81,083 people died in Canada from apparent drug poisonings. According to the CDC's National Center for Health Statistics, there were approximately 107,543 drug overdose deaths in the USA in 2022 (CDC, 2024). That number of deaths rose to 112,000 in 2023 (Mann et al., 2023). Likewise, according to the Health Resources and Services Administration (HRSA), on average, over 130 people per day died from opioid-related overdoses in the USA in 2023 (Health Resources & Services Administration, 2018).

The Slippery Slope of Addiction

Teens often experiment with drugs without realizing how quickly this experimentation can lead to addiction. It's common for teens to believe that they can try a drug once and walk away unscathed, but many substances are highly addictive, and even casual use can spiral into dependency. Opioids, prescription painkillers, and heroin, for example, can lead to addiction after just a few uses (RN, 2024).

Explain to your teen that addiction doesn't happen overnight but can creep in slowly, making it harder to recognize before it's too late. Share real-life stories of those who tried drugs once or twice and ended up battling lifelong addiction. Many teens respond better to real-world examples, especially if you can connect the lesson to someone in your community or a public figure they admire. These examples can drive home the reality that addiction can happen to anyone, regardless of their background, goals, or intentions.

The Long-Term Health Consequences

It's also important to inform your teen about the long-term health effects of drug use. Experimenting with drugs during the teenage years, when the brain is still developing, can have lasting impacts on cognitive function, memory, and emotional regulation. This can lead to learning difficulties and mental health problems, such as depression or anxiety, as well as a reduced ability to cope with stress.

Beyond the brain, drug use can severely affect other parts of the body. Long-term drug use can damage vital organs, such as the heart, liver, and lungs. For example, chronic use of inhalants or stimulants, like cocaine, can result in heart attacks, while substances like alcohol and opioids, can lead to liver damage or failure (Anghel et al., 2023). These risks aren't just for long-term users; even experimenting a few times can lead to irreversible harm.

Peer Pressure and Social Consequences

Teens are often swayed by peer pressure; you will need to equip them with the tools to say no. You can help your teen understand that just because "everyone else is doing it" doesn't mean they should. Discuss the social consequences that can come from drug use, such as strained friendships, damaged reputations, and trouble with school authorities or the law.

Additionally, being involved with drugs can lead to severe legal consequences. Many teens don't realize that even possessing small amounts of illegal drugs can lead to criminal charges, which can impact their future opportunities in education and employment.

Encourage Open Communication and Support

The key to preventing drug experimentation is fostering open communication between you and your teen. Make sure they know that they can come to you with questions, concerns, or situations involving peer pressure without fear of judgment. Offering support and guidance rather than punishment can make them more likely to confide in you if they ever find themselves in a difficult situation involving drugs.

By staying informed and having honest, empathetic conversations with your teen, you can help them make informed decisions about their health and future.

Helping Your Teen Break Free From Drug Addiction

If your teen is already struggling with drug addiction, it's important to remember that all hope is not lost. Recovery is possible with the right support and guidance. As a parent, you play a major role in helping your teen break free from the hold that drugs have on them. The first step is understanding where your teen stands and whether they are willing to seek help. From there, you can create a plan of action that will provide them with the tools they need to regain control of their lives.

Determining Your Teen's Willingness to Quit

The first question to ask is whether your teen is ready and willing to break free from their drug addiction.

Sometimes, teens may not recognize how deeply they've fallen into addiction, or they may be resistant to change. If your teen isn't ready to quit, it's time to have an honest conversation about the harmful effects that drugs are having on their life. This is not the time to sugarcoat the situation; they need to understand the impact of their choices.

For example, ask them if they've noticed how their schoolwork has suffered since they started using drugs. Often, drug addiction can lead to poor concentration, missed assignments, and declining grades. Point out specific examples of how their academic performance has changed, as this can be an eye-opener for teens who may not fully realize the extent of the problem.

Additionally, discuss how their behavior might set a bad example for younger siblings. If your teen has younger brothers or sisters, remind them that their actions are being closely watched and that their choices could influence their siblings. This will help them view their addiction from a different perspective and feel a sense of responsibility for making better choices, not just for themselves but for the family as well.

Finally, it's important to talk about how your teen has been paying for their drug habit. Has your teen been using money from an allowance, selling personal belongings, or even stealing? These are serious conversations to have, especially if they have resorted to illegal activities to fund their addiction. Help them recognize that continuing on this path can lead to legal trouble or strained relationships with family and friends.

Seeking Professional Help

If your teen is willing to break free from drugs, the next step is to determine whether they need professional help. Addiction can be a difficult battle to fight alone, and depending on the substance and the severity of the addiction, professional treatment may be necessary. Some teens may be able to stop using drugs with the support of family and friends, while others may need the guidance of a counselor, therapist, or rehabilitation program.

Reaching out to a doctor or addiction specialist can help assess the level of care your teen needs. For some teens, outpatient therapy may be enough, where they can attend counseling sessions while still living at home and going to school. For others, a more intensive approach like an inpatient rehabilitation center, may be required, especially if the addiction is severe or if the teen has attempted to quit before but has relapsed.

As a parent, showing unwavering support throughout this process is very important. Let your teen know that getting help is not a sign of weakness but a brave step toward recovery. Addiction is not something they should have to handle alone, and it's okay to ask for help.

Once you've begun the process of getting your teen the help they need, it's important to continue providing emotional support. Recovery is a long journey, and there will be moments when your teen struggles or feels like giving up. Stay patient and remind them of the progress they've made, no matter how small.

By keeping the lines of communication open and being there every step of the way, you can help your teen move forward toward a healthier, drug-free future.

Assessing Your Teen's Efforts to Break Free From Drugs

When it comes to addressing your teen's drug addiction, understanding their attempts to quit is also helpful. It can give you insight into their mindset, struggles, and the support they may need moving forward. The journey to recovery is often filled with ups and downs, and recognizing whether your teen has tried to break free from drugs, either successfully or unsuccessfully, can guide your next steps as a parent.

Has Your Teen Tried to Quit?

Begin by having an open conversation with your teen about their experiences with drugs and their efforts to quit. Ask direct questions, like, "Have you ever tried to stop using drugs?" or "What have you done so far to cut back?" Their answers will provide clarity on whether they've attempted to break free from their addiction.

If your teen shares that they've tried to quit before, ask them about their experience. They may say something like, "I went a week without using, but then I started feeling really anxious and went back to it." This provides valuable insight into their experience and can help you identify patterns. Recognizing triggers, whether emotional, social, or environmental, is important for addressing the underlying causes of their addiction.

If they have tried quitting but have faced setbacks, you should acknowledge their efforts. Encourage them by saying, "It's okay to struggle with this; many people do. What do you think made it hard for you to stick to your goal?" This opens the door for a deeper discussion about their challenges and reinforces the idea that setbacks are part of the recovery journey.

Seeking Professional Help

If your teen has made genuine attempts to quit and has repeatedly failed, it may be time to consider professional help. Acknowledging that they need support can be a challenging step for both you and your teen, but know that it matters for their recovery. Explain to them that seeking help is not a sign of weakness, but a proactive step toward regaining control over their life.

There are many options available for professional support, ranging from outpatient therapy to inpatient rehabilitation centers. If your teen is reluctant, try to find examples of success stories, such as friends or family members who have benefited from professional help. Sharing relatable experiences can make the idea of therapy feel less intimidating.

Consider sharing a story about a mutual friend who sought help and is now thriving. "Do you remember (name) from school? She was struggling with the same issues, and after she got help, she became so much more focused and happy. It might be worth looking into." This shows your teen that recovery is possible and helps reduce any stigma they may feel about seeking help.

If They Haven't Tried to Quit

If your teen indicates that they haven't tried to break free from drugs, this can signify a few things. They may feel overwhelmed by the thought of quitting or believe that they can manage their drug use on their own. In this case, you need to encourage them to take the first steps toward recovery.

Start by discussing the benefits of quitting and the positive changes they may experience, like improved focus in school, better relationships, and overall health. You can also say, "Imagine how great it would feel to wake up every day without feeling the need to use drugs. You could focus on your hobbies and have more energy."

Encourage them to consider setting small goals, such as gradually reducing usage. This approach can make the prospect of quitting feel less daunting. You might suggest, "How about we set a goal for you to cut back a little each week? We can check in together and celebrate your progress."

Supporting Their Journey

Regardless of whether your teen has tried to quit or is still contemplating the idea, your support is vital. Show them that you believe in their ability to overcome this challenge. Reassure them that they're not alone on this journey, and emphasize that your love and support are unwavering, no matter what. By taking these steps, you can create a safe space for your teen to explore their feelings about drug use and recovery.

In conclusion, talking openly about drugs gives your teen the tools to make informed, safe choices. Now, let's turn to the influence of friends. The company they keep can shape their values, decisions, and well-being.

Chapter 7: Choice of Friends

Choosing friends is one of the most significant decisions your teen will make during their formative years. Friendships can greatly influence behavior, attitudes, and even values. As a parent, understanding whom your teen associates with can be instrumental in guiding them toward healthy relationships.

We have already discussed this part in Chapter 03; let us take a detailed look at it once more in this chapter.

Knowing Your Teen's Friends

It's very critical to have a grasp of your teen's social circle. The people your teen spends time with can shape their experiences and choices. You may have noticed your child gravitating toward specific friends, but do you truly know these individuals? Take the initiative to learn about them: their interests, hobbies, and family backgrounds. This doesn't mean you should interrogate your teen about every friend; rather you should create an open environment where discussing friendships feels natural.

Try to incorporate casual conversations into your daily routine. For instance, you can say, "I met Sam's parents at the school event last week. They seem really nice! What do you guys like to do together?" This approach not only fosters communication but also signals to your teen that you care about who they choose to be around.

Getting to Know Their Friends' Parents

Just as it's important to know your teen's friends, it's equally vital to connect with their parents. Establishing relationships with other parents can provide valuable insights into their values and parenting styles. This connection can also help you gauge how your teen's friends are being raised and whether they align with your family's principles. Consider hosting a casual gathering where parents can meet and discuss topics relevant to their teens. It can be as simple as a coffee morning or a backyard barbecue. During these gatherings, parents can share their experiences, and you might find common ground with others who have similar values or concerns.

Helping Your Teen Assess Friend Influences

Once you have an understanding of your teen's friends and their backgrounds, it's equally crucial to help your teen evaluate the influence these friends have on them. Encourage your child to think critically about their friendships. Ask them questions such as, "How do you feel when you're with your friends? Do they encourage you to do things with which you're comfortable?" You can discuss a recent incident involving peer pressure. For example, if your teen shares that a friend pressured them into skipping school, you will need to discuss the implications. Ask, "How did that make you feel? Do you think that friend respects your choices?" This encourages your teen to reflect on their friendships and consider whether they're genuinely supportive.

Recognizing Positive and Negative Influences

Help your teen identify the characteristics of positive versus negative friendships. Positive friends should uplift and encourage your teen to be their best self, while negative friends can lead them into risky behaviors or make them feel inadequate.

A positive friendship can be one where your teen feels motivated to excel academically because their friend values education. You can say, "I love how you and Mia study together. It's great to see how you support each other in school!" This reinforces the value of healthy friendships.

Conversely, if your teen mentions a friend who encourages skipping class or engaging in risky behaviors, you can guide them in evaluating that relationship. Ask questions that provoke thought, such as, "How do you think those choices might affect your future?"

Encouraging Healthy Friendships

As your teen navigates the complexities of friendship, your guidance is invaluable. Encourage them to seek out friends who share similar values and interests, and remind them that it's okay to distance themselves from friends who don't respect their choices or boundaries. Reinforce the idea that true friends support each other in making positive life choices.

Encouraging Wholesome Friendships

Fostering healthy friendships for your teen can significantly influence their behavior, values, and overall well-being. As a parent, you have the unique opportunity to create an environment that encourages positive interactions among your teen and their friends. This involves not only understanding their social circle but also being proactive in nurturing these relationships.

Create a Welcoming Home Environment

One of the most effective ways to encourage wholesome friendships is to transform your home into a welcoming space for your teen and their friends. By inviting your teen's friends and their parents over for dinner, you not only get to know the people who influence your child's life, but you also help build a sense of community.

For example, you can host a themed dinner night, such as "Taco Tuesday" or a pizza-making evening. This allows everyone to get involved, making the atmosphere lively and fun. You may say to your child, "Let's invite your friends over for dinner this weekend! We can set up a taco bar and let everyone build their own." This will foster camaraderie and give you the chance to observe the dynamics of their friendships in a relaxed setting.

Make Your Home a Safe Haven

Transform your home into a safe haven where teens feel comfortable hanging out. When your house becomes a gathering place for your teen and their friends, you create an environment that allows you to monitor their activities while ensuring they are in a positive setting.

You can set up a designated area in your home with comfortable seating, games, and activities. For instance, a cozy corner with a gaming console, board games, or even an arts-and-crafts station can attract your teen's friends. You may want to say, "Why don't we make this room a game zone? I'll get some snacks and drinks ready!" This encourages your teen to invite their friends over, reducing the likelihood of them seeking out less wholesome environments.

Be Hospitable and Prepared

Being hospitable goes beyond merely providing a space; it's about creating an inviting atmosphere. Keep drinks and snacks on hand for your teen's friends, ensuring they feel welcome when they arrive. Stock up on a variety of options, from healthy snacks to popular treats, catering to different preferences. Consider having a shelf in the pantry or fridge dedicated to snacks that your teen friends enjoy. You can involve your teen in this: "What do your friends like to snack on? Let's make sure we have some of those ready for when they come over." This small gesture can make your home the go-to spot for friendly gatherings, fostering deeper connections among peers.

Organize Sleepovers and Slumber Parties

Sleepovers and slumber parties are fantastic opportunities for your teen to bond with friends in a safe and supervised environment. These gatherings allow friendships to flourish while enabling you to maintain a level of oversight regarding your teen's social interactions. Next time, consider hosting a themed slumber party, such as a movie marathon or a DIY spa night, instead of sending your child to one. As you prepare, involve your kid and ask, "Let's invite a few of your friends over for a slumber party! We can set up a projector in the backyard and watch movies under the stars." This will make for a memorable experience and strengthen their friendships in a fun, relaxed setting.

Promote Positive Friendships

Ultimately, the goal is to foster friendships that align with the values you want your teen to embrace. By actively engaging with their friends, you can help them choose companions who encourage positive behaviors and healthy choices.

Creating a home that serves as a hub for wholesome friendships not only allows you to keep an eye on your teen's social life, but also strengthens the bond you share with your child. You'll be well-positioned to guide them through the complexities of adolescence, ensuring they are surrounded by friends who uplift and inspire them.

By teaching your teen to choose friends wisely, you help them surround themselves with positive influences. In the upcoming chapter, we'll discuss the physical changes that accompany puberty. Open conversations can help your teen navigate these changes with confidence.

Chapter 8: Changes in Your Body

As your child transitions into their teenage years, they're about to embark on a journey filled with physical changes that can sometimes feel overwhelming, daring, or even scary. It's important to remember that these changes are completely natural and a vital part of growing up. However, without the right preparation and guidance, many teens, and even preteens, may feel frightened or embarrassed by what's happening to their bodies.

As parents, your role is to equip them with the understanding and reassurance they need to navigate this exciting yet challenging phase of life.

Understanding Natural Changes

During adolescence, both boys and girls experience significant physical transformations that signal their bodies are maturing. For girls, the onset of menstruation can be one of the most prominent changes. This milestone, often referred to as their "first period," can trigger a range of emotions, from excitement to anxiety. You can help demystify this experience by talking openly about menstruation and ensuring that your daughter feels supported. Share stories of your own experiences or those of women in your family, and let her know it's a normal part of life. Consider preparing a "period kit" with supplies she can keep in her backpack, ensuring that she feels prepared and confident.

Similarly, tell your girls that they will notice changes in their bodies, such as the development of breasts and hips. These changes are often a source of pride but can also lead to insecurities. Encourage your daughter to embrace her unique body shape and help her understand that everyone develops at their own pace. Use positive affirmations and remind her that beauty comes in many forms. You might even suggest that she explore activities like dance, sports, or art, which can help her connect with her body in a positive way.

Boys and Their Transformations

For boys, the changes can be equally important. They'll experience growth spurts, a deepening of their voice, and the growth of body hair—changes that can happen seemingly overnight. These transformations can feel awkward, especially when they find themselves taller than their peers or suddenly need to face conversations about hygiene and body care. If you approach these topics with humor and openness, you can help them overcome embarrassment, awkwardness, or guilt. For example, you might have a light-hearted chat about the "struggles" of dealing with new facial hair or the oddity of waking up with a wet dream. Reassuring your son that these changes are perfectly normal and experienced by many young men can help alleviate any embarrassment he may feel.

Encouraging your son to take pride in his physical changes is also something you should work on. Engage him in discussions about fitness and nutrition, emphasizing the significance of a healthy lifestyle. This can also be an opportunity to bond, whether it's through cooking healthy meals together or participating in sports or outdoor activities. Let him know that taking care of his body is part of becoming a responsible young adult.

Ultimately, you need to help him embrace these changes as they come. Let him know that his body is evolving into something incredible, and with that evolution come new opportunities and experiences. Instead of viewing these changes with fear, assist him in thinking of them as steps toward becoming the person he is meant to be.

Embracing Privacy: A Teen's Need for Space

As your child navigates the sometimes tumultuous waters of adolescence, one of the most noticeable shifts will be their desire for privacy. Suddenly, the little kid who used to share everything becomes a teenager who may want to keep certain aspects of their life under wraps. This longing for privacy is not only normal; it's an indication of their development. Understanding this need and responding to it with empathy can help strengthen your relationship during this transitional time.

The Importance of Personal Space

If possible, consider giving your teen their own bedroom. Having a space that they can call their own allows them to express their individuality, foster independence, and create a sanctuary where they can unwind after a long day. It doesn't have to be a huge or elaborate room; even a small, cozy space filled with their favorite things can make a world of difference. Encourage your teen to decorate it in a way that reflects their personality, whether through posters, photos, or color schemes. This act of personalizing their space can boost their confidence and give them a sense of ownership.

While having their own room can be incredibly empowering, it's also vital to remind your teen that privacy comes with responsibility. You can have clear conversations about keeping the room tidy or ensuring they manage their time well, emphasizing that they are in charge of this space. By doing this, you are teaching them valuable lessons about independence and accountability.

Establishing Trust Through Confidentiality

Another aspect of fostering your teen's need for privacy is ensuring they feel safe discussing their thoughts and feelings with you. Make it clear that anything shared with you will remain confidential. This assurance can encourage them to open up about sensitive topics, such as their experiences at school, their social life, or any struggles they may face. You might say something like, "I want you to know that if you ever want to talk about something, I'm here to listen, and I will not share it unless you want me to."

An example of this could be when your teen comes to you feeling anxious about a breakup or peer pressure. Instead of reacting in a way that might make them feel judged, let them talk freely. By providing a judgment-free zone, you demonstrate that you respect their privacy and value their feelings. This can lead to deeper conversations and strengthen your bond.

Finding the Balance

While respecting their need for privacy is essential, it's also important to strike a balance. You still need to be aware of what's going on in their lives, especially regarding friendships, school performance, and overall well-being. Encouraging open dialogue can help here. You can ask politely, "I trust you, and I know you're growing up. But I would like to check in from time to time, just so I know you're doing okay." This approach reassures your teen that your intentions are rooted in love and concern, not control.

Remember, it's natural for teens to test boundaries and seek independence. Encourage them to communicate their feelings about privacy and don't shy away from discussing your own need for some boundaries as a parent. For example, you can always mention that you need to feel comfortable knowing they're safe when they go out with friends.

Facilitating Open Conversations: The Power of Shared Experience

Meanwhile, you need to create a space for open discussions about these natural transitions with your teens. One effective way to do this is to arrange one-on-one time with your child. Whether during a walk, a car ride, or a special outing, these moments of solitude can foster a sense of security that encourages candid conversations.

The Comfort of Same-Sex Discussions

When it comes to discussing sensitive topics related to body changes, emotions, and relationships, teens often feel more at ease talking to a parent of the same sex. For instance, a daughter may find it easier to open up to her mom about menstrual cycles, while a son may prefer discussing physical changes and peer pressure with his dad. Understanding this dynamic can help you tailor your approach to facilitate more meaningful conversations.

Consider setting up regular "check-in" times when you and your teen can sit down and talk without distractions. These conversations don't always have to be formal; even casual chats while running errands or enjoying a meal together can lead to valuable discussions. You can offer your help by saying, "I know this can be a confusing time, and I want you to know I'm here for you whenever you feel like talking."

Sharing Your Own Experiences

One of the most powerful ways to connect with your teen is by sharing your own experiences during adolescence. When you recount your awkward moments, fears, or struggles, it humanizes the experience and demonstrates that everyone goes through similar challenges. For example, you can recall how nervous you felt during your first school dance or how awkward you felt when your body began changing.

This sharing can make your teen feel understood and validated. You can also say something like, "I remember feeling really self-conscious when my body started changing, and it was tough to navigate those feelings. It's totally normal to feel that way." This approach will help your kid understand that these experiences are a normal part of life.

Normalizing the Experience

Assure your teen that the physical and emotional changes they are experiencing are completely normal. Many teens worry they are alone in their feelings or that their experiences are unusual. By normalizing these changes, you help remove some of that anxiety.

Encouraging your teen to express their feelings—whether they're anxious, confused, or even excited—

can help them process what they're going through. Create an environment where they feel safe sharing their concerns without fear of judgment. If they express worries about body image or fitting in, listen attentively and validate their feelings. You can respond with, "It's okay to feel that way; a lot of people do. What's important is how you see yourself."

Building a Supportive Atmosphere

In addition to sharing your experiences and reassuring your teen, consider incorporating educational resources. Books, articles, or videos that address adolescent changes can be useful conversation starters. Encourage your teen to ask questions and express any worries they might have after engaging with this material.

It's also helpful to remind them that they're not alone on this journey. Tell them that they can seek support from trusted friends, family members, or even school counselors.

Shopping Together: A Bonding Experience

As your teen embarks on the journey of self-discovery and physical changes, there's no better way to support them than by accompanying them on shopping trips for new personal items. This isn't just about picking up essentials; it's a wonderful opportunity to bond, reassure your child, and help them feel more comfortable during this transformative stage of life.

Supporting Girls: A Visit to the Store

For girls, shopping for bras and sanitary products can feel very strange, especially if they're experiencing these changes for the first time. Think of a time when your daughter walked into a store filled with rows of undergarments and feminine hygiene products—how did she feel? Your daughter might have felt overwhelmed, awkward, or even embarrassed. As her same-sex parent, your presence can make all the difference.

Start by making the shopping trip light and fun. Before heading to the store, you can say, "Let's make this a fun day out! We'll grab lunch afterward, too." This helps ease any anxiety she may have about the experience. When you're in the store, take the time to explain the different types of bras and why they're important for support and comfort. If she feels awkward picking out items, encourage her by saying, "You can choose whatever feels right for you; this is all about your comfort and style."

When it comes to sanitary products, this is a great time to talk openly about periods and what to expect. Reassure her that it's perfectly normal to have questions or concerns. You can say, "I remember my first time too—it can be a bit strange, but you'll get the hang of it."

Guiding Boys: The Essentials

Boys, on the other hand, have their own set of shopping needs as they hit puberty. Whether it's buying their first razor or athletic supporters for sports, your support can make these transitions smoother. Just as with girls, approach the shopping experience with a positive attitude.

Before heading out, say, "Let's check out some cool razors and sports gear! It'll be fun to find what works best for you." In the store, talk about the importance of grooming and how it's a part of looking and feeling good. You can tell them, "Learning to shave can be a bit tricky at first, but it gets easier with practice. You'll be a pro in no time!"

When shopping for athletic supporters, discuss the reasons why they are important for physical activity. You can explain how they provide support and prevent injury during sports. Let him take the lead in choosing what he feels comfortable with, reinforcing that this is his time to make decisions about his body and personal care.

A Fashion Adjustment: Updating the Wardrobe

As teens grow, their styles evolve, too. It may be time for a wardrobe update that reflects their changing tastes and personalities. Consider taking your teen shopping for clothes that not only fit them better but also express who they are becoming.

This can involve helping them pick out clothes that are appropriate for their age and activities while also embracing their unique style. Let them hear, "Let's look for some outfits that are comfortable but still stylish. It's important that you feel good in what you wear." Encourage them to choose colors and styles that make them feel confident.

To make this experience even more enjoyable, you can also turn it into a fashion show at home, where they can model their new outfits for the family. This builds excitement and helps them feel proud of their choices.

This knowledge empowers your teen to feel comfortable in their own body. Our next topic—peer pressure—is often uncomfortable but crucial for today's teens to acknowledge in a safe and informed way.

Chapter 9: Peer Pressure

Peer pressure is an undeniable reality in the lives of teens, shaping their decisions, behaviors, and even their self-esteem. Every day, your teen faces the challenge of balancing their individuality with the desire to fit in with their friends. It's a delicate dance, and understanding the dynamics of peer pressure is crucial for you as a parent.

As a parent, understanding the weight of peer pressure on your teen is key to helping them face these challenging situations. While you can't always shield them from it, you can empower them to make decisions based on their values, rather than just on what their peers expect.

The Need to Be Accepted

It's completely natural for teens to want acceptance and respect from their peers. After all, fitting in during these formative years often feels like the most important thing in the world. They want to be liked, to be seen as cool or fun, and sometimes that means they'll feel pressured to engage in activities they might not normally consider.

For example, a teen may feel compelled to join in on risky behavior, like drinking or smoking, just to avoid being labeled as "boring" or "different." This is where your guidance becomes a guiding light. Remind your teen that real respect doesn't come from following the crowd but from having the courage to stand firm in their values.

Focus on maintaining open communication with your teen. Let them know that it's okay to feel the pull of peer pressure, but it's also perfectly acceptable—and even more admirable—to resist it when it doesn't align with who they truly are. Help them practice responses to situations where they feel pressured, giving them with the tools to navigate these challenges with confidence.

With your support, your teen can learn that true friendships are based on mutual respect, not on conforming to unhealthy behaviors.

Navigating Peer Pressure: Questions for Reflection

Peer pressure can be a tricky landscape for your teen to move, and as a parent, you can help them develop the skills to critically assess their social circles. Encouraging your teen to consider specific questions about their relationships with peers can be a powerful way to foster self-awareness and strengthen their ability to resist negative influences. Let's explore some thought-provoking questions they can ask themselves.

Reflecting on Influences

Start by guiding your teen to consider whether their peers are encouraging them to engage in activities that could be harmful. Questions like, "Are my friends pushing me to try drugs, skip school, or engage in risky behaviors?" can help them recognize if they are in a potentially damaging environment. For instance, if their friends are planning to shoplifting or skipping class to hang out, they must acknowledge that these actions carry serious consequences—not just in terms of punishment, but also for their well-being.

Honesty in Friendships

Next, prompt your teen to evaluate the level of honesty and openness in their friendships. Ask, "Are my peers open and honest with their parents about what we're doing?" This question can lead to valuable insights. If their friends are secretive or frequently lie to their parents about their whereabouts, it may be a sign that the relationship is not built on a foundation of trust and respect.

Sharing an experience might help here: consider a scenario where your teen's friend often claims to be at a "study group" but is actually at a party. If this behavior raises red flags for your teen, it's a sign to reassess the friendship and its impact on their own values and decisions.

The Pressure to Deceive

Encourage your teen to reflect on whether their friends are pushing them to deceive their parents. Questions like, "Are my peers encouraging me to lie to my parents about our activities?" important to consider. If they find themselves in situations where they feel compelled to fabricate stories or hide the truth from you, they need to recognize this as negative peer pressure.

Share a relatable scenario: imagine your teen feels pressured to tell you they're spending the night at a friend's house, but in reality, they're going to a party where there will be alcohol. This is a major red flag and warrants a serious discussion about the importance of honesty and maintaining integrity, both with themselves and with you.

Additional Questions to Consider
You can also help your teens ask themselves:

- "Do my friends respect my boundaries and choices?"

- "Am I feeling anxious or uncomfortable when I'm with them?"

- "Do I feel like I can be myself around them?"

Each of these questions can guide them in evaluating their friendships. If the answers consistently point to discomfort or coercion, it might be time to reconsider the dynamics of those relationships.

Empowering Decision-Making

Ultimately, the goal of these reflective questions is to allow your teen to make informed decisions about their friendships. Encourage open discussions about their thoughts and feelings regarding peer pressure. Remind them that they have the right to choose friends who respect their choices and support their well-being.

By engaging in these conversations and providing a safe space for your teen to explore their feelings, you're not just helping them navigate adolescence's complexities; you're also equipping them with the tools to forge healthy, positive relationships throughout their lives.

Helping Your Teen Navigate Peer Pressure

Let's break down some effective strategies for helping your teen deal with pressure from their peers:

Anticipate the Problem

The first step in helping your teen handle peer pressure is to anticipate potential problems before they arise. This requires open communication and a proactive mindset. Regularly check in with your teen about their social life and the influences they are facing. Questions like, "How are things going with your friends?" "What are your peers doing?" or "Have you felt any pressure to do things you're not comfortable with?" can provide valuable insights.

For example, if your teen has mentioned that their friends are planning a party where there will be drinking, this presents an excellent opportunity to discuss potential scenarios they may encounter. First, you need to ask, "Do you want to avoid the situation of confronting it?" Afterward, you can say, "It sounds like that could be a tricky situation. Let's talk about what you might do if someone offers you a drink." By anticipating these moments together, you help them feel more prepared and less alone in facing peer pressure.

Think About the Pros and Cons

Once you've anticipated the potential challenges, encourage your teen to weigh the pros and cons of their choices. This critical thinking exercise helps them see the bigger picture and make informed decisions. You might say, "Let's break this down. If you go to that party, what do you think the positives might be? And what are some things that could go wrong?"

Encourage them to ask themselves these questions:

1. "What are the benefits and consequences of engaging in certain behaviors?"

2. "How will they feel if they give in?"

3. "Will I be compromising my own principles?"

For instance, the pros of attending a party can include socializing with friends and having fun. However, on the flip side, they should consider the cons: potential exposure to drugs or alcohol, feeling pressured to conform, or even the disappointment from parents if they find out about risky behavior.

Encouraging this reflective practice helps your teen develop decision-making skills that will serve them well beyond their teenage years. By analyzing the situation together, you reinforce the idea that they have the power to make choices based on their values and goals.

Decide What You Will Do

Once your teen has considered the pros and cons, it's time for them to decide which course of action feels right for them. Remind them that it's okay to say no and that they don't need to justify their decision to anyone else. Let them know, "You have the right to choose what feels comfortable for you, and if that means skipping the party or not engaging in certain activities, that's perfectly okay."

For example, if your teen decides they want to attend the party but are uncomfortable with the idea of drinking, help them come up with a strategy. You can suggest they plan to bring a non-alcoholic drink so they have something to sip on while remaining clear-headed. Alternatively, they can decide to text a friend for support if they feel pressured in the moment.

Likewise, encourage them to ask themselves key questions: "Will I be proud of my decision down the road?" and "How will my parents view my decision?" These reflections will help them.

For instance, if your teen is tempted to skip school to hang out with friends, they need to think about how they would feel about that choice weeks or months later. Would they be proud of their spontaneity, or would they regret missing important lessons? Assure them that their parents' views matter. Sharing their decisions with you is a significant step, and knowing how you might respond can provide them with clarity. Ask them, "What do you think I would say if I knew you were skipping class?" This helps reinforce the importance of being honest and considerate of your feelings.

Also, consider how their peers will react. Will they respect your teen's choice to stick to their values, or will they pressure them further? Empower your teen to think critically about their relationships and whether those friendships genuinely support their well-being.

Urging your teen to be proactive in their decision-making empowers them to take ownership of their choices. This autonomy fosters confidence and resilience, allowing them to stand firm in their values even when faced with pressure.

Here are some questions that you can ask your child to reflect on:"

1. "Will I be proud of my decision down the road?"

2. "How will my parents view my decision?"

3. "Will my peers respect my decision?"

Act on Their Decision

The final step is to help your teen act on their decision. This may involve rehearsing scenarios, role-playing conversations, or even practicing refusal skills. You might say, "Let's practice how you would say no if someone offers you a drink. It can be as simple as, 'No thanks, I'm good with my soda,' or 'I'm not interested in drinking tonight.'"

Reinforce the importance of following through on their decision. If your teen decides not to go to a party because they feel it could lead to negative situations, support that choice wholeheartedly. Tell them that their safety and well-being come first. You can say, "I'm proud of you for making a choice that aligns with your values. Remember, you can always choose to leave a situation that makes you uncomfortable."

If they encounter further pressure, such as comments like "Are you chicken?" it's important to prepare them with responses that reflect their reasoning. They can say, "Yes, I'm scared it will lead to bad choices," or "I don't want to because it doesn't feel right." Alternatively, if a friend challenges them with, "I thought you were too smart for that..." they can respond with confidence, asserting their intelligence by reinforcing their choice. "Exactly! That's why I'm choosing not to."

Is Your Teen Dealing With Bullying?

As a parent, it's heartbreaking to think that your kid might be facing bullying. You may have noticed changes in their behavior that raise concerns. *Does my teen have unexplained bruises or seem to cry at home?* These physical signs can indicate that something deeper is going on. So, pay attention to your instincts. If you feel that something is off, it probably is.

Another red flag can be withdrawal from social interactions. If your once vibrant teen is suddenly avoiding friends or family, it's time to investigate further. The isolation can be a sign of emotional distress. Perhaps they used to love attending school events or hanging out with friends, but now they seem reluctant or anxious. This change in behavior should not be taken lightly.

Recognizing Signs of Distress

Do you notice that your teen has trouble sleeping or frequently experiences nightmares? Sleep disturbances can tell that they are grappling with stress and anxiety related to bullying. They may have mentioned feeling anxious about going to school or have started to express dread about specific classes or social gatherings. These conversations can be subtle, but they are necessary. Validate your teen's feelings and let them know that it's okay to share what's on their mind.

It's very important not to minimize the stress your teen may be facing. You may be tempted to dismiss their concerns as typical teenage angst, but you need to recognize that bullying can have serious implications for their mental and emotional health. Instead of downplaying their feelings, acknowledge their experiences and let them know that their emotions are valid.

Starting the Conversation

Broaching the subject can be challenging, but it's vital. Start by creating a safe space where your teen feels comfortable talking. You might say, "I've noticed some changes in you lately, and I want you to know that I'm here to help." This statement opens the door for conversation without putting them on the defensive. Allow them to express themselves at their own pace.

Ask open-ended questions to encourage dialogue. For instance, "Is there anything happening at school that's bothering you?" or "Are your friends treating you the way you deserve?" Be prepared to listen without judgment. Sometimes, your teen just needs someone to hear them out and support them without trying to fix everything immediately.

Understanding the Nature of Bullying

When discussing bullying, try to determine if it's personal or related to pressure to engage in specific activities. Your teen may be experiencing verbal harassment or exclusion from social circles or feel pressured to partake in activities they are uncomfortable with. If it's personal, it will be helpful to talk through specific incidents they've faced and brainstorm ways to address them. If it's pressure-related, help them explore ways to stand firm in their values.

Let your teen know that they're not alone and that it's brave to seek help. Tell them to reach out to trusted adults, teachers, or school counselors who can provide additional support. You might even share your own experiences with bullying or peer pressure, illustrating that they're not the only ones who face these challenges.

Helping Your Teen Build Self-Esteem and Confidence

When bullying feels personal, it can deeply impact your teen's self-esteem and self-confidence. As a parent, you play a pivotal role in helping them navigate these feelings. Start by asking your teen what features they like about their looks. This may seem simple, but helping them identify their positive attributes can significantly shift their focus from negative self-talk to self-appreciation.

Inquire about their praiseworthy skills or traits. What are they good at? Whether it's sports, academics, or creative pursuits, celebrating these talents can help reinforce their sense of worth. Ask them, "Do you feel worthy of love?" Helping them recognize their inherent value is crucial, especially during challenging times. Additionally, ask if they generally see themselves as successful. Success doesn't always mean being at the top; it can be as simple as achieving personal goals or showing kindness to others.

Consider asking questions about their friendships. "Do you have good friends?" and "Are you a good, reliable friend?" can spark conversations about healthy relationships. Emphasize that real friends uplift and support one another. Encouraging your teen to evaluate their friendships can help them understand what a positive support system looks like, reinforcing the idea that they deserve to be surrounded by people who respect and value them.

Acknowledging Resilience in the Face of Pressure

If your teen is facing peer pressure to experiment with drugs, alcohol, or other risky behaviors, commend them for resisting thus far. This affirmation not only boosts their confidence but also reinforces their decision-making abilities. Remind them that standing firm against negative influences takes courage and strength, qualities that they should be proud of.

Review the steps outlined in the previous chapters that cover strategies for handling peer pressure. It's good to revisit these strategies together, reinforcing the idea that they have tools at their disposal to navigate tricky situations. For example, discussing scenarios where they can practice saying "no" or role-playing different responses can help them feel more prepared and confident when facing pressure in real life.

In addition, take the opportunity to review the appropriate chapters on related topics, such as alcohol, drugs, sex, or even suicide. These conversations can provide a context for the pressures they may be feeling and empower them with knowledge about the risks involved. By discussing the realities of these subjects, you can help your teen make informed choices and understand the importance of their decisions.

Throughout this process, keep the lines of communication open.

The Power of Affirmation

Ultimately, your role is to reinforce their self-worth and remind them that they are not defined by the opinions of others. By empowering your teen to embrace their individuality and celebrate their strengths, you are helping them build a resilient mindset that will serve them well throughout their lives. Guide them to practice self-affirmations, and remind them that they are worthy of love, respect, and happiness. Through this journey, you will not only help your teen cope with bullying and peer pressure, but also equip them with the tools they need to thrive in an ever-challenging world.

By helping your teen recognize and resist negative peer influences, you empower them to stay true to themselves. In the following chapter, we'll tackle the topic of pornography. Teens today are often exposed to it early, so understanding its impact can help them make informed choices.

Chapter 10: Pornography

In today's digital age, pornography is everywhere. It's on our screens, easily accessible through various platforms, and often presented as a normal part of adult life. For many teens, the internet serves as a primary source of information about sex, leading them to stumble upon explicit content that can skew their understanding of intimacy and relationships. Although it is completely natural and okay for young people to be curious about sex, pornography doesn't offer an accurate or wholesome perspective. Instead, it often portrays unrealistic scenarios and expectations, which can create confusion and even harm their views on what a healthy sexual relationship looks like.

As parents, you need to approach this topic with openness and understanding, guiding your teen through the complexities of sexuality while addressing the misleading messages that pornography can convey. Together, we can foster a healthy dialogue about sex that prioritizes respect, consent, and genuine connection.

Dealing With the Complex World of Teen Curiosity

Don't Be Shocked—Curiosity Is Natural

As a parent, it's perfectly normal to feel a rush of emotions if you discover that your teen is viewing pornography. Yet, let's take a step back and recognize that curiosity about sex is a part of growing up. Your teen is in a phase of life where they're exploring boundaries, understanding their bodies, and learning about relationships. This exploration is heightened by the reality of our digital age, where pornography is just a click away. Remember, sometimes they might stumble upon explicit content accidentally while searching for something else or even through social media.

The Reality Check: Pornography Isn't Harmless

It's important to talk with your teen about the impact of pornography on their developing minds. Use relatable scenarios to help them understand the complexities of sexual relationships. For instance, consider a teen who watches a popular series that glamorizes casual hookups. They may begin to think that real-life relationships should mirror what they see on screen: flawless, devoid of emotional depth, and often unrealistic. Let them know that while the images they see may appear thrilling, they don't represent the full spectrum of intimacy and connection found in healthy relationships.

Understanding the Consequences

Now, let's dive into why this conversation is so important. Pornography often stirs up desires and fantasies that your teen may not yet be ready to process. This can lead to confusion and unrealistic expectations about what sex should be like. They may even feel pressure to experiment or engage in behaviors they're not emotionally prepared for.

Think of it like this: your teen's friend insists that they've had an amazing experience with their partner, but it turns out to be more about showing off than true intimacy. This friend can be influenced by what they see in pornography, creating a chain reaction where your teen feels compelled to live up to those exaggerated standards.

The Emotional Toll

It's important to acknowledge the emotional fallout that can come from consuming pornography. Many teens experience feelings of shame, embarrassment, or anxiety when they view it, particularly if they know it's a taboo subject. Encourage open dialogues where they can express these feelings without judgment. Share examples of how even adults can struggle with self-esteem and body image issues as a result of unrealistic portrayals in the media.

Building a Healthy Relationship With Intimacy

As a parent, your role is to help your teen develop a healthy understanding of intimacy. Discuss the importance of communication, consent, and respect in relationships. Offer guidance on how to navigate feelings of attraction and curiosity in a way that promotes emotional well-being.

Encourage them to seek out educational resources that provide accurate information about sex and relationships. Help them understand that genuine connection and love far outweigh what they might see on a screen. It's all about helping them form a realistic perspective on relationships while providing the support they need to explore their sexuality responsibly.

Navigating the world of teenage curiosity about sex can be challenging, but you have the power to guide your teen through this journey. By fostering open conversations and promoting a healthy perspective on intimacy, you can help them build a foundation for respectful and fulfilling relationships.

Encouraging Your Teen to Move Beyond Pornography

Understanding Their Willingness to Change

So, your teen has come to you about their interest in pornography. The first thing to establish is whether they're willing to stop. If they express hesitation, it's vital to engage them in a dialogue about the consequences of consuming pornographic material. Ask open-ended questions that prompt them to think critically about how it can affect their understanding of relationships, self-worth, and intimacy. For example, you could say, "Have you noticed how the relationships portrayed in those videos are often so different from real life?" This encourages them to draw connections and recognize the difference between fantasy and reality.

Reasons Behind Their Hesitation

If they are resistant to the idea of stopping, try to understand their perspective. Sometimes, they may feel that viewing pornography is a form of exploration or a way to learn about sex. In these conversations, gently guide them toward recognizing that pornography can distort their perceptions and create unrealistic expectations.

The Conversation About Consequences

When discussing the potential fallout, focus on how pornography can impact their mental health. Many teens experience feelings of guilt and shame after viewing explicit content, which can lead to anxiety and even isolation. Use relatable examples: "Imagine feeling pressured to act a certain way because of what you saw online. What if that makes you uncomfortable in real-life situations?" Highlighting these emotions can help them realize that stepping away from pornography is not just about avoiding explicit content; it's about fostering a healthier relationship with themselves and others.

If They're Ready to Let Go

If your teen shows a willingness to stop viewing pornography, that's a significant step forward!

Celebrate this decision and work together to create a plan to remove access to pornographic material. Start by cleaning out any books, magazines, or games that could lead to temptation. This step not only helps eliminate triggers but also promotes a sense of control over their environment.

Digital Clean-Up: Taking Action Together

Next, tackle the digital side of things. Offer to help them go through their computers, tablets, and smartphones to delete any pornographic material. This process can empower them as they take ownership of their choices. Guide them to set new boundaries for their online activities. You might say, "Let's create a digital space that reflects your values and what you want for yourself."

Installing Parental Filters: A Proactive Approach

Consider installing parental filters on their devices as an extra layer of protection. While this may feel intrusive at first, frame it as a partnership in their journey toward healthier habits. Let them know that these tools are there to support them, not to control them.

Lastly, emphasize that the journey doesn't end with removing explicit content; it requires constant effort to avoid what is truly harmful.

Embracing Wholesome Activities With Your Teen

If your teen has expressed a desire to step away from viewing pornography, one of the best things you can do as a parent is to help them engage in wholesome activities that foster connection, creativity, and joy. It's about replacing the time they might have spent with screens and explicit content with experiences that are enriching and fulfilling.

Let's explore some actionable strategies to make this transition smoother and more enjoyable for both of you.

Plan an Exciting Family Vacation

One fantastic way to encourage wholesome recreation is by planning a family vacation. This can be an excellent opportunity to bond and create lasting memories. Think about places that will appeal to your teen. It could be a beach resort where they can relax and explore, a national park perfect for hiking and discovering nature, or even a vibrant city filled with culture and activities.

When planning, involve your teen in the decision-making process. Ask them where they would love to go and which activities they would be interested in. These activities can include anything from visiting a thrilling amusement park to explore historical landmarks. Engaging them in the planning process not only empowers them, but also makes them more excited about the trip. For example, if they're passionate about history, consider a vacation to Washington, D.C., where you can explore museums and monuments together.

Quality One-on-One Time

In addition to family vacations, carve out regular one-on-one time with your teen. This can be incredibly impactful in strengthening your relationship and showing that you genuinely care about their interests. Choose activities that allow for connection and conversation. Fishing is a wonderful option; the calmness of the water and the relaxed environment create the perfect setting for open dialogue.

You can say, "Hey, how about we spend a Saturday morning fishing at that lake we love? Just you and me." This simple invitation can mean the world to them. While you're out there, you can talk about their hobbies, their thoughts on relationships, or even their goals for the future. It's an opportunity to reinforce your bond and provide guidance in a relaxed setting.

Something Is Revitalizing

Hiking is another excellent option for quality time. There is something revitalizing about being in nature, and it often leads to meaningful conversations. Look for local trails that offer scenic views or wildlife encounters. Before heading out, pack a backpack with snacks and water and make a day of it. You can say, "Let's conquer that trail this weekend! I've heard the view from the top is amazing."

Alternatively, if your teen enjoys swimming, consider spending a day at the pool or a nearby lake. Activities like kayaking or paddle boarding can be fun and active ways to bond while also providing an outlet for energy.

Encouraging New Hobbies

Another great strategy is to help your teen explore new hobbies or interests. This can range from art classes, sports, or music lessons to community service projects. Help them discover activities that spark their passion and creativity. Perhaps they've shown interest in photography; why not take a class together?

You can also suggest, "I found this photography workshop that starts next week. How about we sign up together? It'll be fun to learn something new!"

Creating a Balanced Lifestyle

As you support your teen in transitioning away from pornography, remember that balance is key. Encourage them to find a mix of social activities, hobbies, and family time that resonates with them. Remind them that it's perfectly normal to seek fulfillment in different aspects of life.

By actively engaging your teen in wholesome recreation, you are not just filling their time; you are building a strong foundation for your relationship and helping them find joy in healthy activities. Celebrate their interests, make time for adventures, and embrace the journey together. Through shared experiences, you'll foster a sense of belonging and love that encourages them to make positive choices moving forward.

Next, we'll explore the importance of setting personal goals. This can help your teen build confidence and find a purpose beyond the influences around them.

Chapter 11: Setting Goals

As you help your teens in different ways, it's important to help them envision a brighter future. Encouraging them to think about where they want to be in five or ten years can spark motivation and give their lives a sense of direction. Goal-setting is not just about achieving success; it's about cultivating resilience, self-discipline, and a clearer understanding of their passions and values.

Let us explore this topic about it in this chapter.

Helping Your Teen Dream Big

Start by sitting down with your teen in a relaxed environment, perhaps during a weekend breakfast or a cozy evening at home. Ask them to envision their future. *What kind of career do they dream of pursuing? Do they see themselves traveling the world, starting a family, or making a difference in their community? Do they want to learn some new skills, such as graphic designing or effective communication?* Encourage them to articulate their dreams, no matter how big or small. The key is to let their imagination run wild without the pressure of practicality just yet.

For instance, if your teen expresses a desire to be an astronaut, engage in a discussion about what steps they might need to take to get there, whether excelling in math and science or participating in related extracurricular activities. This conversation helps them visualize a path while also reinforcing that their dreams are valid and achievable.

Breaking Down Long-Term Goals

Once your teen has identified some aspirations, help them break these down into smaller, more manageable goals. This process can feel less overwhelming and make their dreams feel more tangible. For example, if your teen wants to become a veterinarian, discuss the educational steps required: what classes to take in high school, volunteer opportunities at animal shelters, and internships they could pursue later on.

Encourage Goal Setting

Start by encouraging your teen to write down their goals. This simple act can provide clarity and motivation. Discuss the importance of periodically reviewing these goals to track progress and make adjustments. Ask your teen questions like, "What goals in school right now will support your long-term goals?" This will encourage them to think critically about their current academic choices and how they align with their future aspirations.

You can also say, "If you want to pursue a career in engineering, which math or science classes should you focus on right now?" Helping them connect their present activities to their future ambitions not only clarifies the path ahead but also makes their goals feel more attainable.

Explore Academic Opportunities

Next, delve into the academic courses that can support their long-term career goals. Prompt your teen with questions like, "Are there certain courses in school that will support your long-term career goals?" This can open up discussions about electives, honors classes, or extracurricular activities that align with their interests.

For example, if your teen aspires to be a graphic designer, suggest they take art classes or join a digital media club. This way, they can explore their passion and acquire valuable skills that will benefit them down the road.

Additionally, encourage your teen to reflect on their study habits. Ask, "Can you improve your study habits?" Perhaps they could try studying in shorter, more focused bursts or find a study group for support. All you need is to involve them in a conversation about their current habits and identify areas for improvement. For instance, if they often procrastinate, discuss strategies to tackle assignments earlier.

Develop Personal Traits

Setting personal goals is equally important as academic ones. Lead your teen to reflect on their character and habits by asking, "What personal traits or habits would you like to develop?" Help them to think about qualities that will enhance their overall growth.

Is honesty a value they hold? If your teen has trouble being punctual, you could ask, "Does being on time for scheduled events matter to you? How can you make that a priority?" Discussing these traits will help them recognize the areas they want to improve and encourage self-reflection.

Another crucial aspect is their daily routines. Ask, "Does your teen have a regular sleep schedule?" Sleep is fundamental for maintaining energy and focus, especially for adolescents. Encourage them to create a bedtime routine that ensures they get enough rest.

Utilize Free Time Wisely

Finally, consider how your teen uses their free time. Prompt them with questions like, "Do you constructively use your free time?" It's easy for teens to fall into the trap of mindless scrolling on their devices or spending hours playing video games. You can tell them about different hobbies that they can explore or suggest they engage in volunteer work or sports that align with their interests.

Ask your child, "Does your room reflect the level of organization you want to achieve?" Keeping their space neat and tidy can foster a sense of control and help them develop discipline. If they struggle in this area, brainstorm practical strategies together, such as setting a specific time each week for tidying up.

In conclusion, by guiding your teen through this self-reflective process, you help them build a roadmap to their future. Encouraging them to break down long-term goals into smaller steps, evaluate their academic choices, develop personal traits, and utilize their time wisely will empower them to take actionable steps toward achieving their dreams.

Breaking Away From Unwanted Habits

Now that you have helped your teen understand what they want, why not help them in focusing on how undesirable personal traits or habits can hinder their growth?

Open conversations about these habits can lead to meaningful self-reflection, paving the way for positive change.

Identify Personal Habits

Begin by asking, "What personal traits or habits would you like to break away from?" This question will help them to think critically about their behaviors. It is possible that they may realize they often fall into negative patterns, like excessive phone use or unhealthy eating habits. By articulating these habits, they can take the first step toward making a change. You can also share a relatable story about your own journey in breaking a habit.

Tackle Procrastination

Next, address procrastination, a common hurdle for many teens. Ask, "Does your teen struggle with procrastination?" Discuss specific examples, like putting off homework until the last minute or delaying chores until they become overwhelming. Politely but clearly explain how procrastination affects their stress levels and overall well-being. Offer strategies, like setting small, manageable goals to help them tackle tasks one step at a time. For instance, suggest breaking down a big project into smaller, actionable steps, making it feel less daunting.

Reliability in Responsibilities

Finally, it's important to evaluate reliability, especially regarding responsibilities at home. Prompt them with, "Is your teen reliable in doing chores around the house without being reminded?" This can lead to conversations about accountability and the importance of contributing to the household. If they tend to forget chores, help them create a simple chore chart or set reminders on their phone.

Emphasize that taking responsibility for their actions is a valuable life skill that will serve them well beyond their teenage years.

Exploring New Hobbies

We have talked about exploring new habits before; let us discuss it now in detail. Helping your teen discover new hobbies can be a fulfilling journey for both of you.

It's an excellent way for them to express themselves, develop new skills, make friends, and strengthen their bond. Begin by asking, "Would you like to learn a new hobby?" Encourage them to explore interests they may not have considered before, such as painting, playing a musical instrument, or even joining a sports team.

Remember, it's not just about finding something they're good at; it's about enjoying the process of learning. Share your experiences in trying new things. Perhaps you picked up gardening during the pandemic and discovered joy in nurturing plants. Show them that it's okay to step out of their comfort zone and embrace the joy of discovery.

Mastering Basic Life Skills

As your teen grows, they need to master some basic life skills. Start by evaluating their abilities in the kitchen. Try to have them answer the question, "Can you prepare a meal for the family without help?" Cooking is a very useful skill that fosters independence.

To help them, consider organizing a family cooking night where everyone participates. This can be a fun way to teach them how to make simple dishes, like pasta or stir-fry, while creating cherished memories together.

Next, tackle laundry, an essential yet often overlooked skill. Pose the question: "Do you know how to do laundry?" Teach them the basics of sorting clothes, choosing the right settings, and understanding fabric care. You can even turn laundry day into a bonding experience, with music playing in the background while you guide them through the process.

Building Responsibility With Babysitting

Babysitting can be a fantastic opportunity for your teen to build responsibility and gain valuable experience. Ask, "Can you responsibly babysit for younger children?" This skill not only helps them learn about childcare but also enhances their ability to manage situations and communicate effectively with both children and parents.

You can also give them an idea to volunteer for family, friends, or neighbors who need babysitting help. You can assist them in preparing a simple babysitting checklist, including activities to keep younger kids engaged. This way, they'll feel more confident stepping into this role.

Managing Money Wisely

Another essential skill your teen should develop is managing money responsibly. Pose the question, "Do you manage your money well?" Discuss budgeting, saving, and the importance of distinguishing between needs and wants.

You can also set up a small allowance system where they can practice budgeting their money for outings or purchases. Likewise, share your own money management strategies, perhaps explaining how you saved up for that concert ticket when you were younger. Real-life examples will help your teen understand the importance of financial literacy.

The Benefits of a Part-Time Job

Finally, discuss the possibility of your teen having a part-time job or working during the summer months. Ask, "Would you benefit from having a job?" A part-time job teaches them the value of hard work and offers real-life experiences that can enhance their resumes.

Help them find job opportunities that align with their interests. For instance, if they love animals, they can look for a position at a local pet store or animal shelter. Alternatively, they can consider retail or food service jobs that offer valuable interpersonal skills.

Working also provides a sense of independence, as they earn their own money. Remind them that their first job doesn't have to be perfect; it's about gaining experience and learning what they enjoy or don't enjoy.

Encouraging your teen to explore hobbies, master life skills, and take on responsibilities prepares them for adulthood. It's all about fostering independence while maintaining open lines of communication. As they begin this journey, remind them that it's okay to make mistakes; that's how we learn and grow. Your support and guidance will empower them to embrace these experiences confidently.

The Power of Time Management

The ability to prioritize tasks and create a balanced schedule can lead to reduced stress and increased productivity, both in school and beyond, as we all know. Ask yourself: *Would your teen benefit from managing their time better?*

Creating a Summer Schedule

Summer is an excellent opportunity for your teen to practice time management skills. Encourage them to create a summer schedule filled with a mix of responsibilities and enjoyable activities. Help them brainstorm activities they want to pursue during the summer. It can be anything, such as reading, volunteering, or even learning a new skill like coding or photography.

Once they have a list, guide them in breaking it down into a weekly or daily schedule. A colorful planner or a digital calendar can make this process feel exciting! Remind them that the schedule isn't just about chores; it's a way to ensure they make time for the things they love while still being productive.

Sticking to the Schedule

While creating the schedule is a great start, sticking to it is where the real progress happens. Encourage your teen to treat their schedule like a commitment. Share your own experiences with them.

If they find it challenging to adhere to their schedule, suggest that they set small, achievable goals and reward themselves for sticking to them. Perhaps if they follow their schedule for a week, they can treat themselves to a movie or a day out with friends.

Setting boundaries around content helps your teen approach this topic responsibly. Now, we'll look at sex which can be a difficult subject to initiate, but crucial nonetheless to your teens safety and well being.

Chapter 12: Sex

As a parent, it's important to stay informed about the realities of adolescent sexuality. You might be surprised to learn that children as young as eleven and twelve years old are engaging in premarital sex. In some regions, they can even obtain birth control without parental consent. This reality can feel daunting, but it underscores the importance of open communication within the family.

That is why you need to be extra cautious about your child's health.

Your Role in Sexual Education

While you may think that schools or government programs will take the lead in educating your teen about sex, the truth is that you are their most significant resource. Relying solely on external authorities is not enough. Your teen needs to hear from you about the complexities of relationships, consent, and sexual health.

Don't shy away from these conversations. Approach the topic with an open mind and a non-judgmental attitude. For example, if you come across a news story about teen pregnancy or a popular song with sexual themes, use it as a springboard to talk about the responsibilities that come with sexual activity. You can say something like, "I read an article about teen relationships, and it made me think about how important it is to talk about sex and relationships openly."

Your goal is to equip your teen with the knowledge and skills they need to make informed choices. Discuss the importance of consent, understanding emotional connections, and protecting their sexual health. Share your values and encourage them to think critically about their choices.

The world around them may seem confusing and overwhelming, but your guidance and support can help your teen navigate this pivotal time in their lives. You are their first teacher in understanding relationships, love, and responsibility, and that foundation is invaluable as they grow.

Encouraging Chastity: A Path to Emotional and Physical Safety

As parents, you need to guide your teen through the complexities of relationships and sexuality. Encourage them to remain chaste until marriage; it is not just about adhering to traditional values; it is also about protecting their emotional health and physical safety. The world they're navigating can be overwhelming, filled with pressures and influences that may not always prioritize their well-being. Your support and guidance can help them make choices that align with their best interests.

When discussing the importance of chastity, it's essential to approach the topic with understanding and empathy. Start by reasoning with your teen about the potential consequences of premarital sex. Nothing works better than a polite tone mixed with facts and reasoning. You can say something like, "I know that relationships can feel really intense at your age, but it's important to think about the long-term implications of those choices."

Emotional Scars and Broken Hearts

One significant consequence to discuss is the emotional impact of premature sexual experiences. Ask them, "Have you thought about how you might feel if a relationship ends after you've shared something so personal?" This question encourages them to consider the emotional risks involved.

The thrill of a new relationship can quickly turn into heartbreak if things don't work out. Help your teen understand that intimacy often leads to deep emotional connections and a breakup can leave lasting scars.

The Reality of Unwanted Pregnancy

Another good point is the reality of unwanted pregnancies. The statistics can be sobering, and teens must recognize that while they may feel invincible, life can take unexpected turns. Share real stories or show them some meaningful movies that revolve around this topic. This approach personalizes the message and helps your teen see the potential reality rather than abstract statistics.

The Health Risks: STIs and Lifelong Illnesses

Additionally, discuss the health risks associated with premarital sex. Venereal diseases, including HIV and herpes, can have lifelong consequences that extend beyond physical health (Ghebremichael & Finkelman, 2013). Help your teen understand that engaging in sexual activity carries a responsibility for their health and well-being. A conversation can look like this: "It's essential to think about protecting yourself and your future. There are real risks involved, and it's worth considering how those could impact your life down the road."

The Impact of Promiscuity and Reputation

It's also important to address the societal implications of promiscuity. Engaging in casual sexual encounters can lead to a reputation that may be hard to shake. Motivate your teen to think about how they want to be perceived by their peers and the world. Ask them, "What kind of person do you want to be known as? How do you think your choices will affect your reputation?" This reflection can empower them to make decisions aligned with their self-image and values.

Likewise, you can gently remind your teen, "Sometimes, when people jump into relationships or sexual encounters too quickly, it can lead to judgments from others. Have you thought about how you want to be seen by your peers?" This isn't about shaming your teen; it's about helping them understand the societal implications of their choices.

Building Self-Respect and Self-Esteem

One of the most profound reasons to encourage chastity is the preservation of self-respect and self-esteem. When teens engage in sexual activities before they're emotionally ready, it can lead to feelings of regret and diminished self-worth. Reinforce the idea that their value isn't tied to their sexual experiences but rather to their character, choices, and relationships. Encourage them to set standards for themselves and seek relationships built on mutual respect and genuine connection.

Open the Door for Discussion

Remember that these conversations shouldn't be a one-time event but an ongoing dialogue. Foster an environment where your teen feels comfortable discussing their feelings and thoughts about relationships and sexuality. Let them clearly hear, "I'm always here to talk about anything you're feeling or questioning. There's no judgment, just support." This approach reinforces trust and shows your teen that you genuinely care about their well-being.

By encouraging your teen to consider the emotional and physical implications of premarital sex, you're helping them build a strong foundation for their future relationships. Remind them that it's okay to wait and that true love and intimacy will come in time.

Navigating the Pressure: Understanding Consent and Choice

When it comes to the topic of sex, one of the most effective conversations you can have with your teen is about pressure. Always approach this topic with openness and understanding, creating a safe space for your teen to express their feelings and concerns. Start by asking them directly: "Do you ever feel pressured into having sex?" This simple question can open the door to a deeper discussion about their relationships and the influences they face.

Recognizing Peer Pressure

Many teens experience pressure from their peers, often leading them to feel they must conform to certain expectations regarding sex (Widman et al., 2016). You can look at Chapter Nine once more to understand the impact of peer pressure, as it can help you frame this conversation. You might say, "It's not uncommon for friends to talk about sex in ways that can make you feel like you have to join in, even if you're not ready. Have you ever felt that way?" This acknowledgment can help your teen feel seen and understood, making it easier for them to share their own experiences.

The Role of Friends

Don't forget to touch on the importance of friendships, as discussed in Chapter Seven. Encourage your teen to think about the values of their friends. Ask, "Are your friends supportive of your choices, or do they pressure you into things you're not comfortable with?" This helps them evaluate whether their friends are genuinely good influences in their lives or if they may be steering them in a direction that doesn't align with their values.

Understanding the Implications of Birth Control

Now, let's address a topic that can spark strong feelings: birth control. Many parents face the dilemma of whether to offer their teen access to birth control as a form of protection. Undoubtedly, your intention may be to keep them safe, but you need to understand that providing birth control can be seen as giving tacit approval for premarital sex. Simply ask yourself; *offering birth control can send a message that I am okay with them being sexually active. How do I feel about that?*

This will help you understand what you want.

Fostering Self-Respect and Self-Esteem

Most importantly, encourage your teen to prioritize self-respect and self-esteem at all costs. Help them realize that their worth is not tied to their sexual experiences or flings.

Help them focus on true values by asking questions like:

1. What qualities do you admire most in yourself, and how do they contribute to your sense of self-worth?

2. In what ways do you feel appreciated by others, and how does that impact your overall self-esteem?

3. How do you define success, and how does that definition align with your personal values?

4. What activities or relationships bring you the most joy, and how do they influence your perception of yourself?

5. How do you believe your beliefs and values shape your personal identity, and how does that affect your interactions with others?

This reflection can empower them to make decisions that enhance rather than diminish their self-worth.

Ultimately, your goal is to empower your teen to make informed choices that reflect their values and beliefs. By discussing the pressures they face, the implications of sexual activity, and the importance of self-respect, you're helping them navigate the complexities of relationships with confidence. Your support and guidance will enable them to resist peer pressure and make decisions that align with their true selves. Next, we will tackle the subject of smoking.

Chapter 13: Smoking

As the sun set on another busy day, Ayla sat on the porch, watching her teenage son, Jake, fidget with a new vape he had brought home. She recalled her own struggles with smoking and the way it had wrapped its tendrils around her life, choking off her better choices. She understood the weight of the conversation ahead. Discussing smoking with her teen felt daunting, particularly because she had never fully conquered her own battle with tobacco. However, this dialogue was crucial, not just for Jake but for their relationship.

By confronting her own past, Ayla hoped to guide Jake toward healthier choices. Admitting her challenges with smoking didn't make her a hypocrite; instead, it positioned her as a guiding beacon. Sharing her experiences and the consequences of addiction might illuminate a clearer path for Jake, empowering him to make safer decisions while recognizing that honesty and vulnerability can foster genuine understanding.

Talking to your teen about smoking can be tough, especially if, as a parent, you smoke or use tobacco. It may feel hypocritical to advise your teen to steer clear of cigarettes or vaping, but this is one of the most important conversations you can have. It's never too late to be a role model in your teen's life, even if that means acknowledging your own struggles with smoking. Your honesty can go a long way in helping them avoid making the same mistakes.

So, let us break it down below:

Acknowledge the Reality of Smoking

If you smoke, start by being honest with your teen. Say something like, "I know I smoke, and I wish I didn't. I want better for you." This opens the door for an honest conversation and shows your teen that you understand how hard it can be to quit, but that you're trying to do what's best for both of you. Teens are more likely to listen when they see you're not just telling them what to do but sharing your own experiences and concerns.

Review the Facts Together

One of the most effective ways to approach this conversation is by reviewing the facts about smoking and vaping. Let your teen know that it's not just about bad breath and smelly clothes; serious health risks are involved. Smoking and vaping can cause life-threatening diseases and conditions that no one wants to deal with. For example:

- **Mouth, throat, and lung cancer:** Explain that smoking is one of the leading causes of these types of cancer (Hobbs, 2023). You can say, "I know you've probably heard this before, but people die from cancer because of smoking. It's not a scare tactic; it's the reality."

- **Reduced lung capacity:** Tell them, "If you're into sports or even just staying active, smoking will make it harder to breathe. It can affect your performance on the field, in the gym, or even when you're just hanging out with friends." Relating this to something they care about makes it more personal. They will have to deal with reduced lung functionality (Hobbs, 2023).

- **Increased stress and mental health issues:** Smoking doesn't just hurt your body; it also affects your mind. Teens today already face high levels of stress, and smoking only makes it worse(Hobbs, 2023). Share, "You may think smoking will calm you down, but it actually increases stress, anxiety, and panic attacks over time."

The Impact on Relationships and Self-Image

Teens care about how they're perceived by others, and smoking or vaping can impact their relationships and self-esteem. Ask your teen, "How do you want others to see you? Do you want to be the person who can't go without a cigarette or vape, or do you want to be someone who's in control of their life and health?" By framing the conversation around their identity and future, you can encourage them to think long-term.

Secondhand Smoke: Protecting the People Around Them

One often-overlooked consequence of smoking is the impact on others through secondhand smoke. Many teens are empathetic and may not realize that their smoking habits can harm friends, family, or even pets. Share the facts: "Secondhand smoke is dangerous to everyone around you, especially younger siblings, parents, or anyone with asthma or breathing issues. It's not just about you; instead, it's about everyone who's in your space."

Talking About Vaping

Vaping can seem less harmful to teens because of how it's marketed. Be clear about the dangers of vaping, especially since it's often seen as a "healthier" alternative to cigarettes. E-cigarettes contain nicotine, which is highly addictive and can disrupt brain development in adolescents, leading to concentration and behavioral issues. Nicotine exposure at a young age can also prime the brain for addiction to other substances (Fletcher, 2024).

Beyond nicotine, vaping devices emit aerosols containing harmful chemicals, like formaldehyde, acrolein, and diacetyl, which have been linked to respiratory diseases. Inhalation of these substances can irritate the lungs, leading to chronic bronchitis and "vaper's cough," characterized by shortness of breath and wheezing. The long-term effects of vaping are still being studied, but early findings suggest an increased risk of cardiovascular issues, such as high blood pressure, due to chemicals that affect blood vessels (Fletcher, 2024).

Explain, "Vaping is not safe. We're still learning about the long-term effects, but what we do know is that it can lead to lung disease, nicotine addiction, and even more serious health problems down the line. Just because it doesn't have the same smell as cigarettes doesn't mean it's harmless."

Encourage Open Dialogue

Rather than turning this conversation into a lecture, invite your teen to share their thoughts. Ask, "Do your friends vape or smoke? Have you ever been curious about trying it? How do you feel when you're around people who smoke?" By asking questions, you show that you're interested in their perspective and open to a real dialogue. Teens are more likely to listen when they feel heard.

Be a Support System

If your teen is already smoking or vaping, don't panic. The goal isn't to make them feel guilty or ashamed but to help them find a way out. Offer your support by saying, "If you're struggling with this, I'm here to help. It's not easy to quit, but we can find resources and work through it together." There are many quit programs and strategies available, and having you in their corner can make all the difference.

Leading by Example

Finally, if you smoke or use tobacco, consider using this as an opportunity to quit alongside your teen. You can say, "I'm going to try to quit, too. Let's work on this together so we can both be healthier." This not only strengthens your bond but also shows your teen that you're serious about health and wellness. It's never too late to be a positive influence, and your effort to quit can serve as motivation for your teen to avoid starting.

If you discover that your teen is already smoking or vaping, it's normal to feel concerned, even overwhelmed. But remember, this is an opportunity for you to step in as a guide and support system. It's important to handle the situation with care and understanding rather than anger or frustration. Your teen may feel ashamed or may not realize the full impact of their decision. By having open, honest conversations and offering support, you can help them make the best choice for their health.

Step 1: Determine If Your Teen Is Willing to Stop

The first step is to find out where your teen stands. Are they willing to stop smoking or vaping, or are they reluctant? This can be a tough question to ask, but it's important to have this conversation. Begin by saying something like, "I know you've started smoking (or vaping), and I'd like to talk about how it's affecting you. Are you thinking about stopping, or is it something you want to continue?" This opens the door for an honest discussion without making them feel attacked.

If your teen is not willing to stop, it's time to talk about the harmful effects of smoking or vaping. It's important to approach this in a non-judgmental way, focusing on the impact it's having on their life.

Asking the Right Questions

Try to ask specific questions that encourage your teen to reflect on the consequences of their choices. For example:

- **Has their schoolwork suffered since they started smoking?** Smoking and vaping can affect concentration and motivation. If your teen's grades have dropped, it's worth pointing out how their habits could be playing a role. "I've noticed your grades slipping a bit. Do you think smoking is affecting your ability to focus in school?"

- **Have their sleep habits suffered?** Nicotine is a stimulant, which means it can interfere with sleep (Fletcher, 2024). If your teen is staying up later or having trouble falling asleep, ask them, "Have you noticed you're not sleeping as well since you started smoking or vaping?"

- **Are they setting a bad example for their siblings?** If your teen has younger siblings, this can be a powerful motivator. You might say, "Do you think your younger brother or sister looks up to you? How would you feel if they started smoking because they saw you doing it?"

- **How have they been paying for cigarettes or vaping supplies?** Smoking and vaping can be expensive habits. If your teen doesn't have a job, they're likely finding ways to pay for it, which might be concerning. Ask, "Where are you getting the money for cigarettes or vape pods? Have you had to borrow or even steal money to afford them?"

These questions aren't meant to shame your teen but to help them think about the broader impact of their choices. The goal is to guide them toward making healthier decisions for themselves.

Step 2: Determine If They Need Help

If your teen is willing to stop smoking or vaping, the next step is to determine whether they need help quitting. It's important to ask if they've tried to quit before and, if so, what challenges they faced.

Start by asking, "Have you tried quitting before?" This opens up the conversation for them to share their experience if they have one. If they've tried and failed, it's very important to validate their effort while helping them understand that quitting isn't always easy. You could say, "It's great that you've already tried to stop. Quitting can be really hard, but I'm here to help you get the support you need."

In some cases, if they've tried to quit and haven't succeeded, it may be necessary to involve a doctor or healthcare provider. A physician can provide guidance, resources and possibly prescribe nicotine replacement therapies, such as patches or gum, to help your teen manage withdrawal symptoms. You can reassure them by saying, "There's no shame in needing help. We can talk to a doctor about ways to make quitting easier."

Step 3: Helping Them Quit on Their Own

If your teen hasn't tried quitting before, they may be able to do it on their own with your support. However, quitting smoking or vaping often requires more than just willpower. You can help by creating a plan together. Encourage them to set a quit date and offer your assistance in any way they need. "Let's set a date together for you to quit. I'm here for you every step of the way, whether you need someone to talk to or help finding resources."

Developing a Quit Plan

A solid quit plan can make a world of difference. Here are a few steps to consider:

- **Set a quit date:** This gives your teen a goal to work toward. It's helpful to choose a date that's not too far away, so they stay motivated, but far enough to mentally prepare for the change.

- **Identify triggers:** Encourage your teen to think about situations that make them want to smoke or vape. *Is it when they're with certain friends? When they're bored? During stressful moments?* Help them come up with strategies for avoiding or managing these triggers.

- **Find alternatives:** Suggest that they discover healthier ways to cope with stress or boredom, such as exercising, taking up a hobby, or spending time with friends who don't smoke or vape. "What do you enjoy doing that doesn't involve smoking? Maybe we can find some new activities that help take your mind off the habit."

- **Seek support:** Let your teen know they don't have to do this alone. Whether it's through you, a friend, or a support group, having someone to talk to can make the process easier.

Step 4: Lead by Example

Finally, if you smoke or use tobacco, this is a great opportunity to quit alongside your teen. You can say, "I know I've been smoking for years, and it's not easy to quit, but I want to try, too. Let's support each other." Your willingness to take this journey with them can strengthen your bond and show them that quitting is possible, even for long-time smokers.

Step 5: Offer Your Unconditional Support

Quitting smoking or vaping can be a long and difficult journey, especially for teens who may not yet fully grasp the long-term consequences of their choices. The most important thing you can do as a parent is to be a source of unconditional support. Let them know, "I'm proud of you for taking this step, and I'll be here no matter what."

If they slip up or relapse, don't punish or criticize them. Instead, remind them that quitting is a process and that it's okay to make mistakes along the way. "Quitting is hard, and it's okay if you slip up. What's important is that you keep trying. We'll get through this together."

Know that as a parent, helping your teen quit smoking or resist the temptation to start is one of the most empowering things you can do for their health. It's not just about preventing the physical damage that smoking can cause, but also about supporting your teen's emotional strength and self-discipline. Encouraging your teen to remain resolute in their decision not to smoke can make all the difference.

But how do you do that effectively? It starts with providing understanding, guidance, and a strategy in which your teen feels involved.

Encourage Your Teen to Stay Resolute in Their Decision Not to Smoke

The first step is to help your teen stay firm in their decision to either quit or avoid smoking altogether. Remind them that it's okay to feel pressure or temptation, but what matters is how they respond to it.

Tell them how happy and proud you are by saying something like, "I'm proud of you for recognizing how harmful smoking can be, and it takes a lot of strength to stay firm in your decision not to do it. You've got this."

Encourage Your Teen to Write Down Their Reasons for Not Smoking

There's something powerful about putting thoughts into writing. Suggest that your teen jot down their reasons for not smoking or quitting. This can help solidify their resolve and provide a reminder to turn to whenever they feel tempted.

You can say, "Why don't you take a few minutes to write down why you don't want to smoke? You could keep it in your room or even on your phone to look at when you're feeling unsure." Some reasons may include wanting to stay healthy, avoiding addiction, saving money, or preventing long-term health effects like cancer or heart disease. By writing it down, your teen creates a tangible list of reasons to stay strong.

Commend Your Teen for Being Honest and Seeking Your Support

If your teen has been honest about their smoking or desire to quit, you must commend them for their bravery. Quitting smoking or admitting to smoking in the first place can be tough for teens who fear judgment. Let them know you're proud of their honesty.

You should say something like, "It took a lot of courage for you to come to me and tell me what's been going on. I'm really proud of you for that, and I want you to know that I'm here to support you 100%." This will help your teen feel valued and supported, making them more likely to open up about their struggles and seek your guidance in the future.

Encourage Your Teen to Set a Quit Date

Setting a specific quit date is a great way to turn an intention into action. It gives your teen something to work toward and makes the goal feel more achievable.

Encourage your teen by suggesting, "Let's pick a day for you to quit. It doesn't have to be tomorrow, but let's make it soon enough to keep you motivated. What do you think about next weekend or the start of the next school break?" Having a clear goal and timeline helps make the process feel more manageable.

Help Your Teen Get Rid of All Cigarettes, Lighters, Matches, and Ashtrays

Once your teen has set a quit date, it's important to help them get rid of anything that might tempt them to smoke again. Go through their room, their car, or any other spaces where they might stash cigarettes, lighters, matches, or ashtrays.

Frame it as a positive, fresh start by saying, "Let's get rid of all the smoking stuff. You don't need it anymore, and it'll feel good to clear it out. It's like wiping the slate clean." By removing these items, you're helping your teen avoid temptation during moments of weakness.

Remind Your Teen That Withdrawal Symptoms Are Temporary, but the Rewards Are Permanent

Quitting smoking isn't easy, and your teen will likely experience withdrawal symptoms. These can include irritability, anxiety, cravings, and trouble concentrating (Fletcher, 2024). It's beneficial to remind your teen that while these symptoms are tough, they are temporary and will pass. What's important is the long-term benefit of staying smoke-free.

You can say, "I know it's going to be hard for a little while, but remember that these feelings won't last forever. In fact, in a few weeks, your body will already start feeling healthier, and you'll be so glad you stuck it out. The short-term pain is nothing compared to the lifetime of good health you're gaining."

Help them understand the science behind it: nicotine withdrawal symptoms peak after a few days but diminish within a couple of weeks. Remind them of the permanent rewards, such as improved health, more energy, better concentration, and the financial savings that come from not buying cigarettes.

Encourage Your Teen to Avoid Situations and People That Will Tempt Them to Smoke

One of the hardest parts about quitting smoking is avoiding social situations that encourage smoking. Whether it's hanging out with certain friends or going to parties, your teen may need to make some temporary adjustments to their social life.

Guide them on how to react in these scenarios: "You might need to avoid hanging out with friends who smoke for a little while until you feel stronger in your decision. Maybe you can suggest doing something else together, like going to the movies or playing a sport, where smoking isn't involved."

Also, encourage your teen to practice saying no in a way that feels comfortable for them. They can use humor or be direct (whatever works best for their personality). The key is for them to feel confident in their choice.

Celebrate Small Wins Along the Way

It's important to celebrate the milestones in your teen's journey to quitting smoking, no matter how small they may seem. Whether it's going a day, a week, or a month without smoking, acknowledge their efforts and remind them how proud you are of their commitment.

In the next chapter we will discuss time management as it relates to your teens use of social media and digital technology.

Chapter 14: Social Media

Social media is an integral part of your teen's life, but it's also one of the trickiest landscapes for parents to navigate. While it offers exciting opportunities for connection and creativity, it also carries risks that can have long-lasting consequences. As parents, helping your teen understand and appreciate these risks cannot be neglected to ensuring they engage with social media in a healthy and responsible manner.

In this chapter, we'll explore how you can talk to your teen about the potential dangers of social media and how they can protect themselves.

Help Your Teens Appreciate the Risks Associated With Social Media

Your teen may be tech-savvy, but that doesn't always mean they're aware of the risks involved in posting online. Social media can seem like a fun and carefree space to share thoughts and photos, but what happens online doesn't always stay there. It's important to help your teen appreciate that the decisions they make on social media today can impact their future.

Once Something Is Posted, It Can't Be Permanently Erased

One of the most critical points to convey to your teen is the permanence of what they post. Teens often act impulsively, and social media gives them a platform where these impulses are captured forever. Whether it's a photo they later regret or a heated comment they wish they could take back, once something is out there, it's impossible to erase it entirely.

Politely suggest your teen think before they post by saying something like, "Before you post that picture or comment, ask yourself: Would I be okay with my future boss or college admissions officer seeing this? If the answer is no, it's probably best to skip it."

Remind your teen that even if they delete a post, someone else may have already taken a screenshot or shared it. For example, if a teen posts a fun yet inappropriate photo with friends, that photo can resurface and affect their chances when applying for a job or scholarship. The internet has a long memory, and it's very important they understand this before making decisions they may regret later.

Private and Personal Information Is Out There for Anyone to Access

Another risk to highlight is the amount of private and personal information teens can unknowingly share on social media. From posting about their vacation plans to tagging their location, they may be giving away more than they realize. Teens may not always understand that sharing this information could expose them to unwanted attention or even danger.

Use real-life examples to make this point. For instance, explain, "Imagine you post that your family is going on a week-long vacation. You're excited and want to share it with friends, but now, anyone who sees that post knows your house will be empty. It's like sending an open invitation to burglars."

Help them understand that even if their social media accounts are set to "private," not everyone who sees their posts may have good intentions. Strangers, hackers, or people with malicious intent can access personal information and use it against them.

You can also teach them how to use the privacy settings on their accounts wisely and to think carefully about who they allow into their digital world. Reinforce the message that they don't need to share everything with everyone.

Teach Your Teen About Digital Footprints

A useful concept to introduce to your teen is the idea of a digital footprint. Every time they post, comment, or like something online, they're leaving behind a trace of their online activity. This footprint can be used by future employers, colleges, or even strangers to learn more about them.

Encourage your teen to be mindful of the footprint they're leaving behind by saying, "Everything you do online, whether it's commenting on a friend's post or sharing a meme, creates a picture of who you are. Make sure it's a picture you're proud of and one you'd be happy for anyone to see."

Cyberbullying and Online Harassment Are Real Threats

Although social media can offer positive interactions, it's also a breeding ground for cyberbullying and online harassment. Unfortunately, many teens experience bullying in the form of cruel comments, public shaming, or being excluded from online social circles.

Talk to your teen about the reality of cyberbullying and how to handle it if they or someone they know becomes a target. You can say, "If anyone is ever unkind to you online, don't engage with them. Save the messages and come to me or tell a trusted adult so we can figure out the best way to respond."

Let them know that they are not alone and that there are steps they can take, such as blocking the person or reporting the behavior to the platform. Ask them to support friends who may be experiencing online bullying as well.

Social Media Can Impact Mental Health

Spending excessive time on social media can take a toll on your teen's mental health. Constantly comparing themselves to the curated, filtered lives of others can lead to feelings of inadequacy, low self-esteem, and even depression (Zubair et al., 2023). Teens can easily get caught up in the "highlight reel" of other people's lives, forgetting that social media rarely shows the full picture.

Help your teen keep perspective by saying, "Remember, what you see on social media is usually the best version of someone's life. People don't post about their struggles, bad days, or failures as much. So, don't feel like you have to measure up to the perfection you see online."

You can ask them to maintain a balance by suggesting offline activities, such as spending time with family, going for a walk, or pursuing a hobby. This can help them disconnect from the pressures of social media and focus on what truly matters.

Encourage Positive Social Media Use

While there are risks, social media can also be a powerful tool for good. Encourage your teen to use their platforms for positive purposes, such as staying connected with family and friends, supporting causes they care about, or showcasing their talents.

You might say, "Social media can be a great way to make a difference. Why not share something inspiring, support a friend, or raise awareness about something you believe in?"

Teach them to think critically about what they consume online and to question the information they come across. Not everything on social media is accurate or helpful, and it's essential to teach your teen how to distinguish between reliable sources and misinformation.

Set Boundaries and Screen Time Limits

As a parent, setting boundaries around social media use is also important. This doesn't mean you need to ban it entirely, but creating guidelines regarding when and how much time they spend online can help prevent unhealthy habits.

For example, you may suggest no phones at the dinner table or limiting social media use before bedtime to help them sleep better. Explain your reasoning by saying, "I know you love connecting with friends online, but we also need to make sure it doesn't interfere with other parts of your life, like family time or getting enough sleep."

By establishing clear rules, you can help your teen strike a healthy balance between their online and offline lives.

Is Your Teen Addicted to Social Media or the Internet?

As a parent, it's easy to feel concerned about your teen's screen time and whether it has become an unhealthy obsession. In today's digital world, social media, online games, and smartphones have become such a central aspect of life, making it challenging to distinguish between normal use and addiction. However, there are clear signs to watch for, and helping your teen find a healthy balance is crucial.

In this section, we'll explore how to assess whether your teen's internet and social media habits are becoming problematic, as well as what you can do to guide them toward healthier habits.

How Much Time Does Your Teen Spend on Their Devices?

One of the first things you can do is take a closer look at how much time your teen is spending on their phone, computer, or gaming console. *Are they spending hours texting, posting pictures, scrolling through TikTok or Instagram, or playing electronic games?* While some screen time is normal, excessive use can be a sign of a deeper issue.

Ask yourself: How many hours per day is my teen engaging with electronic media? Are they spending more time online than participating in other important activities, such as sports, hobbies, or spending time with family and friends?

For instance, if your teen used to love playing basketball after school but now spends all their free time glued to their phone, this could be a red flag.

It would be helpful to initiate a conversation with your teen to gain their perspective. You can say, "I've noticed you've been spending a lot of time on your phone lately.

How do you feel about it? Do you think it's taking away from other things you enjoy?"

Does Your Teen Neglect Other Activities?

Another critical sign of potential addiction is whether your teen is neglecting other activities in favor of engaging with electronic media. *Are they missing out on social events, physical activities, or even sleep because they can't put their phone down?*

For example, does your teen stay up late watching YouTube videos or playing video games, then struggle to get up for school the next day? If so, it's time to step in. Lack of sleep and neglecting personal interests can take a toll on their physical health, emotional well-being, and academic performance.

Help your teen find a balance by encouraging them to take breaks from their devices and engage in other activities they enjoy. It's good to frame this conversation positively rather than making them feel guilty or ashamed, as discussed earlier.

Has Your Teen's School Performance Suffered Since Getting a Smartphone?

A sudden drop in academic performance is one of the most telling signs that your teen may be overusing their smartphone or the internet. If your teen's grades have slipped, or if teachers are raising concerns, it may be worth investigating whether their screen time is getting in the way of their schoolwork.

You can ask questions like, "Have you been struggling to keep up with your assignments since you've started spending more time online?" Sometimes, teens may not even realize how their online habits are impacting their academics, so bringing this up in a gentle and supportive manner can help them reflect on their priorities.

If they admit they're having trouble focusing or getting their homework done because they're constantly checking their phone, work together to set realistic limits. For example, suggest that they put their phone in another room while studying or set specific times for social media use.

Is Your Teen Texting During Meals or Interrupting Conversations?

One of the more subtle signs of social media addiction is how it seeps into everyday life. *Does your teen text during family meals or interrupt face-to-face conversations to check their notifications?* This kind of behavior can be a sign that their online world is taking precedence over real-life interactions.

It's important to help your teen understand the value of being present in the moment and prioritizing in-person connections. You can implement something like, "I love when we have family dinners without distractions. Can we all agree to leave our phones aside during mealtimes?"

Setting clear boundaries around phone use during family time can help your teen disconnect from the digital world and re-engage with the people around them. It's also a good opportunity to model healthy behavior yourself—after all; teens are more likely to follow your lead if they see you making an effort to unplug as well.

Are Teachers Noticing Social Media Use in Class?

If your teen's teachers have mentioned that they're texting in class or seem distracted by their phone, this is another clear sign that social media use may be getting out of hand.

Teens may not fully understand the long-term consequences of this behavior, especially regarding their education. Remind them that their attention should be focused on learning while they're at school and that constant distractions can affect their ability to perform well in exams and secure future opportunities.

Helping Your Teen Find a Healthy Balance

If you're starting to see signs that your teen is becoming too reliant on social media or the internet, it's important not to panic or become overly worried. Instead, approach the situation with positivity, courage, empathy, and understanding. Many teens don't realize they're developing unhealthy habits and simply need guidance in finding balance.

Here are a few practical steps you can take:

- **Set screen time limits:** Establish clear rules about when and how long your teen can use their devices. For example, you can set a rule that phones are turned off an hour before bed to ensure they get enough sleep.

- **Encourage offline activities:** Help your teen rediscover hobbies and interests that don't involve screens. Whether playing sports, painting, reading, or going for a walk, remind them of the joy that comes from offline experiences.

- **Lead by example**: Your teen is more likely to follow healthy tech habits if they see you doing the same. Try setting aside time each day when everyone in the family takes a break from their screens.

- **Open dialogue:** Keep the lines of communication open. If your teen feels pressured to always be online because of their friends or feels overwhelmed by social media, encourage them to talk about it with you. Together, you can come up with strategies to ease that pressure.

Encourage Your Teen to Set Reasonable Limits

Help them recognize that moderation is key. Suggest that they keep track of how much time they spend on electronic media each day. There are even apps that can monitor screen time and help them remain mindful of their usage. Encourage them to set a daily limit that allows time for schoolwork, family activities, and hobbies—helping them stay productive while still enjoying their online lives.

Recognize the Need for Connection

It's important to acknowledge that your teen's desire to stay connected with friends and family is valid. Adolescence is a time when social interactions are particularly meaningful, and online platforms provide a way for teens to maintain friendships, especially during times when in-person contact might be limited.

However, remind your teen that real-life connections and face-to-face conversations are equally important. Help them strike a balance by encouraging activities that allow them to interact with others in person, whether through sports, clubs, or family outings. For example, if they're used to spending hours chatting with friends online, suggest meeting up for a weekend activity like a hike or movie night. This can be a refreshing break from screens while still allowing them to maintain those relationships.

Discourage Gossip and Inappropriate Media Use

The internet can be a breeding ground for harmful behaviors like gossip, cyberbullying, and sharing inappropriate content. It's vital to talk to your teen about the importance of using electronic media responsibly and with kindness.

Encourage them to steer clear of online gossip or conversations that target others. You can explain, "It's easy for rumors to spread online, and once something is out there, it's hard to take it back. How would you feel if someone spread rumors about you?" Encourage your teen to think twice before posting or sharing anything that could hurt someone else's feelings. Lead by example by modeling respectful online behavior yourself.

Similarly, talk to your teen about the dangers of pornography and sexting. This can be an uncomfortable conversation, but it's the need of the hour. Sexting may seem like a private or harmless way to explore their sexuality, but remind them that once a picture or message is sent, it can be easily shared without their consent, leading to long-term consequences. You can gently approach the subject by saying, "I know a lot of teens are exposed to things online that can be confusing. Let's talk about how to stay safe and make sure you're not putting yourself in a vulnerable position."

Ask your teen if they've ever felt pressured to sext or share intimate images. Peer pressure plays a huge role in teen behavior, and they may not always understand the risks involved. Acknowledge the social pressures they may face, but emphasize the importance of protecting their privacy and self-respect.

Is Media Use Impacting Their Schoolwork or Sleep?

It's not uncommon for teens to lose track of time while engaging with electronic media. However, if your teen's schoolwork or sleep patterns are suffering as a result, it's time to step in. Ask your teen questions like, "Have you noticed that your grades have dropped since you started staying up late on your phone?" or "Do you feel tired all the time because you're not getting enough sleep?"

Teens may not always realize the impact that screen time has on their daily lives, so these questions can prompt them to reflect on their habits. Once they recognize the issue, work together to create a plan for healthier media use. Set specific rules for when devices should be turned off.

Explain the benefits of getting enough sleep and staying focused in school, and help them see that setting limits isn't about punishment, but rather about helping them in achieving their goals.

Encourage Accountability: Keeping Track of Screen Time

Encouraging your teen to be aware of their screen time can be an effective way to help them develop better habits. Suggest that they keep a journal or use an app to track how much time they spend on different online activities. This exercise can help them see just how much time is slipping away and motivate them to make changes.

For instance, if they realize they're spending five hours a day on social media, they may decide to cut that down to two hours and use the extra time to work on a personal project, read a book, or pursue a hobby. Setting these goals together can make it a more collaborative process, giving your teen a sense of ownership over their choices.

Sticking to Media Time Limits

Once your teen has set a reasonable limit on their media time, the next step is to encourage them to stick to it. This may require some trial and error; after all, it's easy to get immersed in the digital world. However, you can help by offering positive reinforcement and support.

For example, if your teen successfully limits their screen time for a week, celebrate by doing something fun together, like going out for ice cream or having a movie night. This will show them that their efforts are valued and that there are rewards beyond the virtual world.

Helping Your Teen Create a Balanced Relationship With Media

In today's world, it's unrealistic to expect teens to completely disconnect from electronic media. Instead, the goal should be to help them develop a balanced and mindful relationship with their devices. By setting limits, fostering awareness, and encouraging responsible behavior, you can help your teen enjoy the benefits of technology without letting it take over their life.

Through open communication and consistent support, your teen can learn to navigate the digital world in a way that promotes their well-being, protects their privacy, and encourages them to stay present in the real world. In the next chapter, we'll discuss suicide, a difficult but important topic to ensure your teen knows that they're never alone.

Chapter 15: Suicide

As a parent, the thought of your teen struggling with depression or suicidal thoughts can be overwhelming and heartbreaking. However, it's important to know that open and honest communication can, once again, come to the rescue for both you and your child. If you notice that your teen has been feeling unusually sad or disconnected, reach out immediately. Although discussing mental health or suicide may seem daunting, starting the conversation can be a lifeline for your teen. They need to know that you are there for them, without judgment, and that their feelings matter.

Is There an Apparent Reason for the Sadness or Depression?

When a teen experiences deep sadness or depression, it can sometimes be linked to specific life events, such as struggles at school, conflicts with friends, or the loss of a loved one. However, there are also times when there may be no clear reason for their emotions. In either case, it's vital to take their feelings seriously and offer them the space to express what's on their mind.

You can gently ask, "Is there something going on that's making you feel this way? I've noticed that you haven't been yourself lately." Keep your tone calm and compassionate, showing them that you're genuinely concerned, not just about their behavior but also about their well-being.

If they open up about a particular issue, resist the urge to immediately offer solutions. Often, teens just need to know someone is listening. Simply saying, "That sounds really tough. I'm here for you, no matter what," can provide immense comfort.

If your teen isn't able to pinpoint a specific cause for their depression, reassure them that it's okay not to have all the answers right now. Sometimes, emotions are complex, and the reasons behind them aren't always easy to explain. What matters most is that they don't feel alone in dealing with their feelings.

Assure Your Teen You've Noticed a Change in Their Mood

One of the first steps in supporting your teen is to let them know you've observed changes in their mood and behavior without sounding accusatory or confrontational. You can say something like, "I've noticed you've been really down lately, and it seems like something is bothering you. I just want to check in and see how you're feeling." This type of statement is nonjudgmental and shows that you care.

Your teen may initially deny that anything is wrong, but don't let that deter you from continuing to be present for them. Even if they don't want to talk right away, knowing that you've noticed and care enough to ask makes an impact.

The Problem Won't Go Away, But Talking About It Helps

Teens often feel that the problems they're dealing with are insurmountable. A failed relationship, bullying at school, or even a low grade on an important test can feel like the end of the world to them. They may believe that their pain will last forever and that there's no way out of their situation.

This is where your role as a parent becomes vital. Encourage your teen to talk about what's troubling them, even if you can't immediately fix the problem. By talking, they may begin to gain a new perspective or at least feel some relief from the weight they've been carrying.

Talk to them by saying, "I know it feels like there's no solution right now, but talking about it could help you feel less overwhelmed. Let's take it one step at a time."

Helping them break down the situation into smaller, more manageable pieces can make the problem feel less daunting.

If they're reluctant to talk, remind them that you're not expecting to solve everything all at once. "We don't have to figure it all out right now," you can say, "but I'd love to understand what's going on so I can be there for you."

Assure Your Teen That Their Privacy Will Be Respected

Teens are often hesitant to open up to their parents because they fear their private thoughts and struggles will be shared with others. Assure your teen that whatever they tell you will remain confidential unless there's a serious risk to their safety.

Reassure them by saying, "I promise that whatever we talk about stays between us unless I'm really worried about your safety. In that case, I'd need to get extra help to keep you safe. But other than that, you can trust me." Establishing this trust is key to creating a safe environment where your teen feels comfortable opening up.

You can also remind them that their feelings are valid, no matter how "big" or "small" they may seem. If your teen feels like their issues aren't significant enough to talk about, encourage them by saying, "There's no problem too small. If it's bothering you, it's important, and I'm here to help you through it."

Remind Your Teen That Time Brings Change

One of the most powerful messages you can share with your teen is that their current struggles, no matter how overwhelming, are temporary. When a teen is in the depths of depression, it can be hard for them to see beyond the present moment. They may believe that the way they feel now will last forever, which can contribute to suicidal thoughts.

Offer them reassurance by saying, "I know things feel really heavy right now, but things will change. Life is full of ups and downs, and what you're feeling now won't last forever." Share examples from your own life, if appropriate, of times when you faced difficult situations that eventually improved. Personal stories can make the idea of change more relatable and give them hope.

Help them understand that emotions fluctuate and that they won't always feel the way they do now. This isn't meant to minimize their pain but rather to give them hope for the future.

Do Mental Health Problems Run in Our Family?

Family history can play a huge role in mental health. Conditions like depression, anxiety, and bipolar disorder can sometimes have genetic links. If you or other family members have experienced mental health challenges, it's time to acknowledge this possibility with your teen. By doing so, you not only normalize the conversation but also help them understand that they are not alone in their struggles.

You can say something like, "I've noticed that we have a history of mental health issues in our family. I want you to know that if you're feeling overwhelmed, it's not your fault. We can talk about it and find help together." This approach fosters an environment in which your teen feels safe to share their feelings without fear of judgment.

Consider Seeking Professional Help

If you recognize patterns of mental health issues in your family, it may be time to seek professional help. Many mental health conditions can improve significantly with proper treatment. Therapy, medication, and support groups are just a few options that can make a real difference in your teen's life.

Encourage your teen by saying, "There's no shame in asking for help. Many people, including myself, have sought professional guidance at different points in their lives. It's a sign of strength to take that step." This assurance can alleviate some of the stigma associated with seeking help, empowering them to take charge of their mental health.

Remind Your Teen: There Is No Shame in Seeking Medical Help

Your teen needs to understand that seeking medical help for mental health concerns is not something to be ashamed of. Society has come a long way in recognizing the importance of mental health, yet some stigmas still linger. Your words can help break down these barriers.

You can share a personal story or experience if appropriate, illustrating that mental health challenges are common and that seeking help is a brave choice. For example, you might say, "When I was your age, I felt overwhelmed, too. I reached out to a counselor, and it changed my life for the better. It's okay to talk to someone about what you're feeling." Sharing your own journey shows vulnerability and can inspire your teen to take similar steps.

Understanding the Signs of Struggle

While every teen experiences ups and downs, some signs may indicate a more serious struggle. Look for changes in mood, behavior, and daily routines. Is your teen withdrawing from friends or activities they once enjoyed? Are they exhibiting sudden changes in academic performance? These signs can often point to deeper issues that need to be addressed.

If you notice any concerning changes, don't hesitate to approach the conversation gently. You could say, "I've noticed that you haven't been hanging out with your friends as much, and your schoolwork seems to be slipping. Is everything okay?" This non-confrontational approach allows your teen to open up about their feelings.

Sharing Your Own Challenges

Sharing your own experiences with mental health can be a powerful way to connect with your teen. When appropriate, let them know that everyone faces challenges and that it's perfectly okay to seek help when needed. This can help normalize the conversation and diminish feelings of isolation.

For example, you might say, "I remember a time when I felt really anxious about everything, and I didn't know how to cope. Talking to a therapist helped me a lot. It made me realize that I wasn't alone, and that there were tools to manage my feelings." By sharing your challenges, you can show your teen that it's normal to struggle and that they can come through it.

Building a Support Network

Encouraging your teen to build a support network is crucial. Friends, family, and mental health professionals can all play important roles in their journey toward healing. Help them identify trusted individuals with whom they can talk about their feelings, whether it's a close friend, a favorite teacher, or a counselor.

Creating a Safe Environment

Creating a safe and supportive home environment can come in handy for your teen's mental health. This involves being aware of conversations surrounding mental health and proactively addressing any negative stigmas. Encourage open dialogue about feelings, struggles, and even the everyday stresses of life.

You can establish family check-ins where everyone can share how they're feeling. Say something like, "Let's make it a tradition to sit down once a week and check in with each other. We can talk about what has been good and what has been challenging." This regular practice can foster a sense of community and support within your family.

Encourage Journaling as an Outlet

Writing can be a powerful tool for processing emotions, and encouraging your teen to keep a private journal can help them articulate their feelings. Journaling provides a safe space for self-reflection and can serve as an emotional release.

Suggest to your teen, "Why not try writing down your thoughts and feelings in a journal? It's a great way to clear your mind and understand what you're going through." They may find that putting their thoughts on paper helps them organize their feelings and gain perspective on their challenges.

You can also recommend prompts to get them started, such as:

- What made me happy today?
- What has been bothering me?
- What are my goals for the week?
- What am I thankful for today?

- What new things do I want to try?
- How do I want to spend my free time?
- What am I feeling grateful for right now?
- Who do I want to connect with this week?
- What challenges am I willing to face?

Journaling can be a private and personal experience, allowing your teen to explore their emotions without fear of judgment.

Draw Close to God in Prayer

Spirituality can be a source of strength and comfort for many individuals, especially during challenging times. Encouraging your teen to draw close to God through prayer can provide them with a sense of peace and hope.

You can say, "If you're feeling overwhelmed, taking a moment to pray or meditate can really help. Sometimes, it's comforting to know you're not alone and that there's a higher power you can turn to."

Share relevant scriptures that resonate with themes of comfort and support, such as Psalm 23, which speaks of God's guidance and care, or James 4:8, which encourages drawing near to God. These verses can remind your teen of the strength that faith can provide (Bible Gateway, 2015).

You can suggest, "Try reading a verse that speaks to you or simply talk to God about what you're feeling. It's a way to express your thoughts and seek guidance."

Encouraging Positive Activities

In addition to journaling and prayer, encourage your teen to engage in positive activities that foster emotional well-being. Whether it's participating in sports, pursuing a hobby, or spending time with friends, these activities can provide much-needed relief from stress.

Let your teen know, "It's important to take breaks and do things that make you happy. Let's find something you love to do and make time for it together." This can be anything from painting to hiking, offering them a constructive outlet for their emotions.

Remind Them of Your Unconditional Support

Throughout this process, remind your teen that your love and support are unwavering. Assure them that it's okay to seek help and that they don't have to face their struggles alone.

Tell them, "I want you to know that no matter what you're going through, I'm here for you. We can work through this together." This ongoing support will reinforce your teen's confidence in their ability to navigate their feelings and seek help when needed.

Keeping an open door can make all the difference in helping your teen through dark times. As we conclude, remember that this journey is ongoing, and meaningful conversations will continue to be your most powerful tool.

Conclusion

As we reach the end of this book, let us pause and reflect on the journey you've taken as a parent. The goals outlined in the introduction were designed to guide you in fostering a strong, open relationship with your teen. Let's take a moment to assess your progress in achieving these goals and celebrate the strides you've made in your parenting journey.

One of the primary objectives was to ensure that you are now regularly engaging in meaningful conversations with your teen. Think back to your early interactions: *Were they often filled with one-word responses and eye rolls?* Now, consider the depth of discussions you've cultivated. *Have you noticed a shift? Are your conversations richer, allowing both you and your teen to express thoughts and feelings freely?*

Open communication is not just a one-time effort; it's an ongoing process. By establishing yourself as a good listener, you've likely created an environment where your teen feels comfortable coming to you with their thoughts, challenges, and even their successes. It's a powerful shift when your child seeks you out for advice or simply to share their day. Remember, these moments are the building blocks of a trusting relationship that will serve them well throughout their lives.

You should now feel more equipped to guide your teen through life choices. Reflect on the discussions you've had about the choices they face daily, from academic challenges to social pressures. Your guidance isn't about dictating their decisions, but about helping them weigh options and consider consequences.

Consider how you've instilled moral standards and guidelines for your teen to live by. *Are they beginning to articulate their values? Have you noticed them making choices that align with the principles you've discussed together?* These conversations about ethics and values will stick with them and influence their behavior long after they leave your immediate care.

Another goal was to help your teen combat negative peer pressure. Assess how you've approached this topic. *Have you provided them with the tools to recognize peer pressure and the confidence to resist it?* Reflect on conversations where you explored what real friendship means and how to stand firm in their beliefs, even when faced with challenging social situations.

Encouraging your teen to think critically about their friendships and to choose companions who uplift and support them will significantly impact their self-esteem and decision-making. Remember, it's not just about saying "no" to negative influences; it's about empowering them to choose positive ones.

By now, you should have a clear idea of the important conversations to have with your teen. From discussing sexuality and substance use to exploring their dreams and ambitions, you've likely found ways to address these sometimes uncomfortable topics. Reflect on how you approached these conversations. *Were you open and non-judgmental? Did you create a safe space for dialogue?*

As your teen grows and changes, so will the topics you discuss. Make a commitment to keep these conversations ongoing, adapting as needed to reflect their evolving needs and interests.

Protecting your teen from sex, drugs, alcohol, smoking, pornography, and suicide is a monumental task, but it's one that you should feel more equipped to handle now. *Have you shared factual information about these issues with them in a relatable way? Have you encouraged them to seek help or talk about their feelings if they ever find themselves in distress?*

Your active involvement in their lives is your best defense against the dangers they may encounter. By providing them with knowledge, support, and a safe space to talk, you're not only protecting them, but also teaching them to protect themselves.

Helping your teen set reasonable, positive life goals is another vital objective. *Have you engaged them in discussions about their aspirations, both short-term and long-term?* Reflect on whether you've encouraged them to think about what success looks like for them and how to map out a path to achieve it.

By helping your teen identify their passions and set achievable goals, you're instilling a sense of purpose that will guide them through their teenage years and beyond. Your support and encouragement can help them navigate setbacks and celebrate successes.

Lastly, consider how well you've prepared your preteen for changes in their body. *Have you approached the topic of puberty and development with openness and honesty?* Reflect on how you've fostered a sense of comfort around these natural changes.

Creating a safe space for your preteen to ask questions about their bodies and what to expect is significant. Your candid discussions can help alleviate fears and empower them to embrace these changes with confidence.

As you reflect on these goals and your achievements, remember that parenting is a continuous journey. No one gets it perfect, and challenges will arise along the way. What matters is your willingness to learn, adapt, and grow alongside your teen. By committing to ongoing communication and support, you're not just raising a child; you're nurturing a confident, capable adult who is ready to face the world.

I hope this book has provided valuable insights and practical tools for strengthening communication with your teen. Your feedback is important; please take a moment to share your thoughts and let me know how this guide has helped you. Thank you for reading!

Continue to celebrate your successes, learn from your challenges, and, above all, stay connected with your teen. Know that your relationship is one of the most powerful influences in their life, and the effort you put into it will yield lifelong benefits.

References

Anghel, D.-M. C., Nițescu, G. V., Tiron, A. T., Guțu, C. M., & Baconi, D. L. (2023). Understanding the mechanisms of action and effects of drugs of abuse. *Molecules*, *28*(13), 4969–4969. https://doi.org/10.3390/molecules28134969

Bible Gateway. (2015). *Bible gateway passage: Psalm 23 - new international version.* Bible Gateway; BibleGateway. https://www.biblegateway.com/passage/?search=Psalm%2023&version=NIV

CDC. (2024, November 15). *U.S. overdose deaths decrease in 2023, first time since 2018.* CDC. https://www.cdc.gov/nchs/pressroom/nchs_press_releases/2024/20240515.htm

Courtney, K. E., & Polich, J. (2009). Binge drinking in young adults: Data, definitions, and determinants. *Psychological Bulletin*, *135*(1), 142–156. https://doi.org/10.1037/a0014414

Fletcher, J. (2024, February 16). *Vaping vs. smoking: Long-term effects, benefits, and risks.* Medical News Today. https://www.medicalnewstoday.com/articles/vaping-vs-smoking

Ghebremichael, M. S., & Finkelman, M. D. (2013). The effect of premarital sex on sexually transmitted infections (STIs) and high risk behaviors in women. *Journal of AIDS and HIV Research (Online)*, 5(2), 59. https://pmc.ncbi.nlm.nih.gov/articles/PMC3634578/

Health Resources & Services Administration. (2018, March 22). *Opioid crisis*. HRSA. https://www.hrsa.gov/opioids

Hegde, A., Chandran, S., & Pattnaik, J. I. (2022). Understanding adolescent sexuality: A developmental perspective. *Journal of Psychosexual Health*, 4(4), 263183182211075. https://doi.org/10.1177/26318318221107598

Hobbs, H. (2023, January 6). *Twenty-six health effects of smoking on your body*. Healthline. https://www.healthline.com/health/smoking/effects-on-body

Mann, B., Pattani, A., & Bebinger, M. (2023, December 28). *In 2023 fentanyl overdoses ravaged the U.S. and fueled a new culture war fight*. NPR. https://www.npr.org/2023/12/28/1220881380/overdose-fentanyl-drugs-addiction

RN, S. W. (2024, June 28). Common drug street names: Stay in the know. *Gallus Detox Centers*. https://www.gallusdetox.com/blog/drug-street-names/

Smith, S. (2023, September 20). *Dating vs. relationships: 15 differences you must know about.* Marriage.com. https://www.marriage.com/advice/relationship/dating-vs-relationship/#What_is_dating

The Vibe Team. (2022, May 5). Thirty-five quotes about communication to inspire collaboration. *Vibe.* https://vibe.us/blog/35-quotes-about-communication/?srsltid=AfmBOorT1XLNljgbMMZv47LE7ekBwPLR0sZ0371j4VmNCtqNBYQDcMAE

Widman, L., Bradley, S. C., Helms, S. W., & Prinstein, M. J. (2016). Adolescent susceptibility to peer influence in sexual situations. *Journal of Adolescent Health, 58*(3), 323–329. https://doi.org/10.1016/j.jadohealth.2015.10.253

Zubair, U., Khan, M. K., & Albashari, M. (2023). Link between excessive social media use and psychiatric disorders. *Annals of Medicine and Surgery, 85*(4), 875–878. https://doi.org/10.1097/MS9.0000000000000112

Made in the USA
Columbia, SC
17 January 2025